Mastering Linux Shell Scripting
Second Edition

A practical guide to Linux command-line, Bash scripting, and
Shell programming

Mokhtar Ebrahim
Andrew Mallett

D1592385

Packt>

BIRMINGHAM - MUMBAI

Mastering Linux Shell Scripting
Second Edition

Commissioning Editor: Vijin Boricha
Acquisition Editor: Rohit Rajkumar
Content Development Editor: Ron Mathew
Technical Editor: Prachi Sawant
Copy Editor: Safis Editing
Project Coordinator: Judie Jose
Proofreader: Safis Editing
Indexer: Mariammal Chettiyar
Graphics: Tom Scaria
Production Coordinator: Aparna Bhagat

First published: December 2015
Second edition: April 2018

Production reference: 1180418

Published by Packt Publishing Ltd.
Livery Place
35 Livery Street
Birmingham
B3 2PB, UK.

ISBN 978-1-78899-055-4

www.packtpub.com

`mapt.io`

Mapt is an online digital library that gives you full access to over 5,000 books and videos, as well as industry leading tools to help you plan your personal development and advance your career. For more information, please visit our website.

Why subscribe?

- Spend less time learning and more time coding with practical eBooks and Videos from over 4,000 industry professionals

- Improve your learning with Skill Plans built especially for you

- Get a free eBook or video every month

- Mapt is fully searchable

- Copy and paste, print, and bookmark content

PacktPub.com

Did you know that Packt offers eBook versions of every book published, with PDF and ePub files available? You can upgrade to the eBook version at `www.PacktPub.com` and as a print book customer, you are entitled to a discount on the eBook copy. Get in touch with us at `service@packtpub.com` for more details.

At `www.PacktPub.com`, you can also read a collection of free technical articles, sign up for a range of free newsletters, and receive exclusive discounts and offers on Packt books and eBooks.

Contributors

About the authors

Mokhtar Ebrahim started working as a Linux system administrator in 2010. He is responsible for maintaining, securing, and troubleshooting Linux servers for multiple clients around the world. He loves writing shell and Python scripts to automate his work. He writes technical articles on the Like Geeks website about Linux, Python, web development, and server administration. He is a father to a beautiful girl and a husband to a faithful wife.

> *I would like to thank my wife for helping me with all her efforts to finish this book. Thank you, Doaa, for being a part of that. Also, I would like to thank everyone at Packt for working with me to make sure the book is released. Last but not least, I'd like to thank Brian Fox, the author of the bash shell, for creating such an awesome piece of software; without it, such a book would not exist.*

Andrew Mallett is the owner of The Urban Penguin, and he is a comprehensive provider of professional Linux software development, training, and services. Having always been a command-line fan, he feels that so much time can be saved through knowing command-line shortcuts and scripting. TheUrbanPenguin YouTube channel, maintained by Andrew, has well over 800 videos to support this, and he has authored four other Packt titles.

About the reviewer

Sebastiaan Tammer is a Linux enthusiast from The Netherlands. After attaining his BSc in Information Sciences, he graduated with MSc in Business Informatics, both from Utrecht University. His professional career started in Java development before he pivoted into Linux.

He has worked on number of technologies, such as Puppet, Chef, Docker, and Kubernetes. He spends a lot of time in and around his terminal of choice: bash. Whether it is creating complex scripting solutions or just automating simple tasks, there is hardly anything he hasn't done with bash!

> *I would like to thank my girlfriend, Sanne, for all the help and support she has given me throughout the years. She has had to endure the late nights studying, me fixing stuff (which I had inevitably broken only hours earlier), and my endless storytelling about all those exciting new technologies. Thanks for the enormous amount of patience and love, I could not have done it without you!*

Packt is searching for authors like you

If you're interested in becoming an author for Packt, please visit authors.packtpub.com and apply today. We have worked with thousands of developers and tech professionals, just like you, to help them share their insight with the global tech community. You can make a general application, apply for a specific hot topic that we are recruiting an author for, or submit your own idea.

Table of Contents

Preface

First, you'll learn about Linux shells and why we chose the bash shell. Then, you'll learn how to write a simple bash script and how to edit your bash script using Linux editors.

Following this, you will learn how to define a variable and the visibility of a variable. After this, you will learn how to store command execution output into a variable, which is called command substitution. Also, you will learn how to debug your code using bash options and Visual Studio Code. You will learn how to make your bash script interactive to the user by accepting input from the user using the read command. Then, you will learn how to read options and its values if the user passed them to the script. Following this, you will learn how to write conditional statements such as if statements and how to use case statements. After this, you will learn how to create code snippets using vim and Visual Studio Code. For repetitive tasks, you will see how to write for loops, how to iterate over simple values, and how to iterate over directory content. Also, you will learn how to write nested loops. Along with this, you will write while and until loops. Then, we will move on to functions, the reusable chunks of code. You will learn how to write functions and how to use them. After this, you will be introduced to one of the best tools in Linux, which is Stream Editor. As we are still talking about text processing, we will introduce AWK, one of the best text processing tools in Linux that you will ever see.

After this, you will learn how to empower your text processing skills by writing better regular expressions. Finally, you will be introduced to Python as an alternative to bash scripting.

Who this book is for

This book targets system administrators and developers who would like to write a better shell script to automate their work. Some programming experience is preferable. If you don't have any background in shell scripting, no problem, the book will discuss everything from the beginning.

What this book covers

Chapter 1, *The What and Why of Scripting with Bash*, will introduce Linux shells, how to write your first shell script, how to prepare your editor, how to debug your shell script, and some basic bash programming, such as declaring variables, variable scope, and command substitution.

Chapter 2, *Creating Interactive Scripts*, covers how to read input from the user using read command, how to pass options to your script, how to control the visibility of the entered text, and how to limit the number of entered characters.

Chapter 3, *Conditions Attached*, will introduce the if statement, the case statement, and other testing command such as else and elif.

Chapter 4, *Creating Code Snippets*, covers creating and using code snippets using editors, such as vim and Visual Studio Code.

Chapter 5, *Alternative Syntax*, will discuss advanced testing using [[and how to perform arithmetic operations.

Chapter 6, *Iterating with Loops*, will teach you how to use for loops, while loops, and until loops to iterate over simple values and complex values.

Chapter 7, *Creating Building Blocks with Functions*, will introduce functions and explains how to create a function, list builtin functions, pass parameters to functions, and writing recursive functions.

Chapter 8, *Introducing the Stream Editor*, will introduce the basics of sed tool to manipulate files, such as adding, replacing deleting, and transforming text.

Chapter 9, *Automating Apache Virtual Hosts*, contains a practical example of sed and explains how to create virtual hosts automatically using sed.

Chapter 10, *AWK Fundamentals*, will discuss AWK and how to filter file content using it. Also, we will discuss some AWK programming basics.

Chapter 11, *Regular Expressions*, covers regular expressions, their engines, and how to use them with sed and AWK to empower your script.

Chapter 12, *Summarizing Logs with AWK*, will show how to process the httpd.conf Apache log file using AWK and extract useful well-formatted data.

Chapter 13, *A Better lastlog with AWK*, will show you how to use AWK to output beautiful reports using the lastlog command by filtering and processing the lastlog output.

Chapter 14, *Using Python as a Bash Scripting Alternative*, will discuss Python programming language basics and explains how to write some Python scripts as a bash script alternative.

To get the most out of this book

I assume that you have a little programming background. Even if you don't have a programming background, the book will start from the beginning.

You should know some Linux basics such as the basic commands such as `ls`, `cd`, and `which`.

Download the example code files

You can download the example code files for this book from your account at `www.packtpub.com`. If you purchased this book elsewhere, you can visit `www.packtpub.com/support` and register to have the files emailed directly to you.

You can download the code files by following these steps:

1. Log in or register at `www.packtpub.com`.
2. Select the **SUPPORT** tab.
3. Click on **Code Downloads & Errata**.
4. Enter the name of the book in the **Search** box and follow the onscreen instructions.

Once the file is downloaded, please make sure that you unzip or extract the folder using the latest version of:

- WinRAR/7-Zip for Windows
- Zipeg/iZip/UnRarX for Mac
- 7-Zip/PeaZip for Linux

The code bundle for the book is also hosted on GitHub at `https://github.com/PacktPublishing/Mastering-Linux-Shell-Scripting-Second-Edition`. In case there's an update to the code, it will be updated on the existing GitHub repository.

We also have other code bundles from our rich catalog of books and videos available at `https://github.com/PacktPublishing/`. Check them out!

Download the color images

We also provide a PDF file that has color images of the screenshots/diagrams used in this book. You can download it from `https://www.packtpub.com/sites/default/files/downloads/MasteringLinuxShellScriptingSecondEdition_ColorImages.pdf`.

Conventions used

There are a number of text conventions used throughout this book.

`CodeInText`: Indicates code words in text, database table names, folder names, filenames, file extensions, pathnames, dummy URLs, user input, and Twitter handles. Here is an example: "Edit your script so that it reads like the following complete code block for `$HOME/bin/hello2.sh`"

A block of code is set as follows:

```
if [ $file_compression = "L" ] ; then
tar_opt=$tar_l
elif [ $file_compression = "M" ]; then
tar_opt=$tar_m
else
tar_opt=$tar_h
fi
```

Any command-line input or output is written as follows:

```
$ type ls
ls is aliased to 'ls --color=auto'
```

Bold: Indicates a new term, an important word, or words that you see onscreen. For example, words in menus or dialog boxes appear in the text like this. Here is an example: "Another very useful feature is found on the **Preferences** | **Plugins** tab"

 Warnings or important notes appear like this.

 Tips and tricks appear like this.

Get in touch

Feedback from our readers is always welcome.

General feedback: Email feedback@packtpub.com and mention the book title in the subject of your message. If you have questions about any aspect of this book, please email us at questions@packtpub.com.

Errata: Although we have taken every care to ensure the accuracy of our content, mistakes do happen. If you have found a mistake in this book, we would be grateful if you would report this to us. Please visit www.packtpub.com/submit-errata, selecting your book, clicking on the Errata Submission Form link, and entering the details.

Piracy: If you come across any illegal copies of our works in any form on the Internet, we would be grateful if you would provide us with the location address or website name. Please contact us at copyright@packtpub.com with a link to the material.

If you are interested in becoming an author: If there is a topic that you have expertise in and you are interested in either writing or contributing to a book, please visit authors.packtpub.com.

Reviews

Please leave a review. Once you have read and used this book, why not leave a review on the site that you purchased it from? Potential readers can then see and use your unbiased opinion to make purchase decisions, we at Packt can understand what you think about our products, and our authors can see your feedback on their book. Thank you!

For more information about Packt, please visit packtpub.com.

The What and Why of Scripting with Bash

1

Welcome to the what and why of bash scripting. In this chapter, you will discover the types of shells in Linux and why we chose bash. You will learn what bash is, how to write your first bash script, and how to run it. Also, you will see how to configure Linux editors, such as vim and nano, in order to type your code.

Like in any other scripting language, variables are the basic blocks of coding. You will learn how to declare variables such as integers, strings, and arrays. Furthermore, you will learn how to export these variables and extend their scope outside the running process.

Finally, you will see how to visually debug your code using Visual Studio Code.

We will cover the following topics in this chapter:

- Types of Linux shells
- What is bash scripting?
- The bash command hierarchy
- Preparing text editors for scripting
- Creating and executing scripts
- Declaring variables
- Variable scope
- Command substitution
- Debugging your scripts

Technical requirements

You'll need a running Linux box. It doesn't matter which distribution you use, since all Linux distributions are shipped nowadays with the bash shell.

Download and install Visual Studio Code, which is free from Microsoft. You can download it from here: `https://code.visualstudio.com/`.

You can use VS Code as an editor instead of vim and nano; it's up to you.

We prefer to use VS Code because it has a lot of features such as code completion, debugging, and many more besides.

Install `bashdb`, which is a required package for the bash debug plugin. If you are using a Red Hat-based distribution, you can install it like this:

```
$ sudo yum install bashdb
```

If you are using a Debian-based distribution, you can install it like this:

```
$ sudo apt-get install bashdb
```

Install the plugin for VS Code, called bash debug, from `https://marketplace.visualstudio.com/items?itemName=rogalmic.bash-debug`. This plugin will be used to debug bash scripts.

The source code for this chapter can be downloaded here:

`https://github.com/PacktPublishing/Mastering-Linux-Shell-Scripting-Second-Edition/tree/master/Chapter01`

Types of Linux shells

As you know, Linux consists of some major parts, such as the kernel, the shell, and the GUI interface (Gnome, KDE, and so on).

The shell translates your commands and sends them to the system. Most Linux distributions are shipped with many shells.

Every shell has its own features, and some of them are very popular among developers today. These are some of the popular ones:

- **Sh shell**: This is called the Bourne shell, this was developed at AT&T labs in the 70s by a guy named Stephen Bourne. This shell offers many features.
- **Bash shell**: Also called the Bourne again shell, this is very popular and compatible with sh shell scripts, so you can run your sh scripts without changing them. We are going to use this shell in this book.
- **Ksh shell**: Also called the Korn shell, this is compatible with sh and bash. Ksh offers some enhancements over the Bourne shell.
- **Csh and tcsh**: Linux was built using the C language and that drove developers at Berkeley University to develop a C-style shell in which the syntax is similar to the C language. Tcsh adds some minor enhancements to csh.

Now we know the types of shells and we know that we are going to use bash, so what is bash scripting?

What is bash scripting?

The basic idea of bash scripting is to execute multiple commands to automate a specific job.

As you might know, you can run multiple commands from the shell by separating them with semi colons (;):

```
ls ; pwd
```

The previous line is a mini bash script.

The first command runs, followed by the result of the second command.

Every keyword you type in bash scripting is actually a Linux binary (program), even the `if` statement, or `else` or `while` loops. All are Linux executables.

You can say that the shell is the glue that binds these commands together.

The bash command hierarchy

When working on the bash shell and when you are sitting comfortably at your prompt eagerly waiting to type a command, you will most likely feel that it is a simple matter of typing and hitting the *Enter* key. You should know better than to think this, as things are never quite as simple as we imagine.

Command type

For example, if we type and enter `ls` to list files, it is reasonable to think that we were running the command. It is possible, but we often will be running an alias. Aliases exist in memory as a shortcut to commands or commands with options; these aliases are used before we even check for the file. Bash's built-in `type` command can come to our aid here. The `type` command will display the type of command for a given word entered at the command line. The types of command are listed as follows:

- Alias
- Function
- Shell built-in
- Keyword
- File

This list is also representative of the order in which they are searched. As we can see, it is not until the very end where we search for the executable file `ls`.

The following command demonstrates the simple use type:

```
$ type ls
ls is aliased to 'ls --color=auto'
```

We can extend this further to display all the matches for the given command:

```
$ type -a ls
ls is aliased to 'ls --color=auto'
ls is /bin/ls
```

If we need to just type in the output, we can use the −t option. This is useful when we need to test the command type from within a script and only need the type to be returned. This excludes any superfluous information, and thus makes it easier for us humans to read. Consider the following command and output:

```
$ type -t ls
alias
```

The output is clear and simple, and is just what a computer or script requires.

The built-in type can also be used to identify shell keywords such as if, and case. The following command shows type being used against multiple arguments and types:

```
$ type ls quote pwd do id
```

The output of the command is shown in the following screenshot:

```
pi@pilabs /tmp $ type ls quote pwd do id
ls is aliased to `ls --color=auto'
quote is a function
quote ()
{
    local quoted=${1//\'/\'\\\'\'};
    printf "'%s'" "$quoted"
}
pwd is a shell builtin
do is a shell keyword
id is /usr/bin/id
pi@pilabs /tmp $ _
```

You can also see that the function definition is printed when we stumble across a function when using type.

Command PATH

Linux will check for executables in the PATH environment only when the full or relative path to the program is supplied. In general, the current directory is not searched unless it is in the PATH. It is possible to include our current directory within the PATH by adding the directory to the PATH variable. This is shown in the following command example:

```
$ export PATH=$PATH:.
```

This appends the current directory to the value of the PATH variable; each item in the PATH is separated using a colon. Now your PATH has been updated to include the current working directory and, each time you change directories, the scripts can be executed easily. In general, organizing scripts into a structured directory hierarchy is probably a great idea. Consider creating a subdirectory called bin within your home directory and add the scripts into that folder. Adding $HOME/bin to your PATH variable will enable you to find the scripts by name and without the file path.

The following command-line list will only create the directory, if it does not already exist:

```
$ test -d $HOME/bin || mkdir $HOME/bin
```

Although the preceding command-line list is not strictly necessary, it does show that scripting in bash is not limited to the actual script, and we can use conditional statements and other syntax directly at the command line. From our viewpoint, we know that the preceding command will work whether you have the bin directory or not. The use of the $HOME variable ensures that the command will work without considering your current filesystem context.

As we work through the book, we will add scripts into the $HOME/bin directory so that they can be executed regardless of our working directory.

Preparing text editors for scripting

Throughout the book, we will be working on Linux Mint, and this will include the creation and editing of the scripts. You, of course, can choose the way you wish to edit your scripts and may prefer to make use of a graphical editor, so we will show some settings in gedit. We will make one excursion into a Red Hat system to show screenshots of gedit in this chapter.

Also, we will use Visual Studio Code as a modern GUI editor to edit and debug our scripts.

To help make the command-line editor easier to use, we can enable options and we can persist with these options through hidden configuration files. Gedit and other GUI editors, and their menus, will provide similar functionality.

Configuring vim

Editing the command line is often a must and is part of a developer's everyday life. Setting up common options that make life easier in the editor give us the reliability and consistency we need, a little like scripting itself. We will set some useful options in the vi or vim editor file, `$HOME/.vimrc`.

The options we set are detailed in the following list:

- `set showmode`: Ensures we see when we are in insert mode
- `set nohlsearch`: Does not highlight the words that we have searched for
- `set autoindent`: We indent our code often; this allows us to return to the last indent level rather than the start of a new line on each line break
- `set tabstop=4`: Sets a tab to be four spaces
- `set expandtab`: Converts tabs to spaces, which is useful when the file moves to other systems
- `syntax on`: Note that this does not use the `set` command and is used to turn on syntax highlighting

When these options are set, the `$HOME/.vimrc` file should look similar to this:

```
set showmode
set nohlsearch
set autoindent
set tabstop=4
set expandtab
syntax on
```

Configuring nano

The nano text editor is increasing in importance and it is the default editor in many systems. Personally, I don't like the navigation or the lack of navigation features that it has. It can be customized in the same way as vim. This time, we will edit the `$HOME/.nanorc` file. Your edited file should look something like the following:

```
set autoindent
set tabsize 4
include /usr/share/nano/sh.nanorc
```

The last line enables syntax highlighting for shell scripts.

Configuring gedit

Graphical editors, such as gedit, can be configured using the preferences menu, and are pretty straightforward.

Enabling tab spacing to be set to **4** spaces and expanding tabs to spaces can be done using the **Preferences** | **Editor** tab, as shown in the following screenshot:

You can download the example code files from your account at
`http://www.packtpub.com` for all the Packt Publishing books you have
purchased. If you purchased this book elsewhere, you can visit
`http://www.packtpub.com/support` and register to have the files e-mailed
directly to you.

Another very useful feature is found on the **Preferences** | **Plugins** tab. Here, we can enable the **Snippets** plugin, which can be used to insert code samples. This is shown in the following screenshot:

For the rest of the book, we will be working on the command line and in vim; feel free to use the editor that you work with best. We have now laid the foundations to create good scripts, and, although whitespace, tabs, and spaces in bash scripts are not significant, a well-laid-out file with consistent spacing is easy to read. When we look at Python later in the book, you will realize that in some languages, the whitespace is significant to the language and it is better to adopt good habits early on.

Creating and executing scripts

With our editors primed and ready, we can now move quickly to creating and executing our scripts. If you are reading this book with some prior experience, we will warn you that we are going to start with the basics, but we will also include looking at positional parameters; feel free to move on at your own pace.

Hello World!

As you know, it is almost obligatory to begin with a `Hello World` script and we will not disappoint as far as this is concerned. We will begin by creating a new script, `$HOME/bin/hello1.sh`. The contents of the file should read as in the following screenshot:

```
#!/bin/bash
echo "Hello World"
exit 0
```

We hope that you haven't struggled with this too much; it is just three lines, after all. We encourage you to run through the examples as you read to really help you instill the information with good hands-on practice.

- `#!/bin/bash`: Normally, this is always the first line of the script and is known as the shebang. The shebang starts with a comment, but the system still uses this line. A comment in a shell script has the `#` symbol. The shebang instructs the interpreter of the system to execute the script. We use bash for shell scripts, and we may use PHP or Perl for other scripts, as required. If we do not add this line, then the commands will be run within the current shell; it may cause issues if we run another shell.
- `echo "Hello World"`: The `echo` command will be picked up in a built-in shell and can be used to write a standard output, `STDOUT`; this defaults to the screen. The information to print is enclosed in double quotes; there will be more on quotes later.
- `exit 0`: The `exit` command is a built-in shell, and is used to leave or exit the script. The `exit` code is supplied as an integer argument. A value of anything other than `0` will indicate some type of error in the script's execution.

Executing the script

With the script saved in our `PATH` environment, it still will not execute as a standalone script. We will have to assign and execute permissions for the file, as needed. For a simple test, we can run the file directly with bash. The following command shows you how to do this:

```
$ bash $HOME/bin/hello1.sh
```

We should be rewarded with the `Hello World` text being displayed on our screens. This is not a long-term solution, as we need to have the script in the `$HOME/bin` directory, specifically, to make running the script easy from any location without typing the full path. We need to add in the execute permissions as shown in the following code:

```
$ chmod +x $HOME/bin/hello1.sh
```

We should now be able to run the script simply, as shown in the following screenshot:

```
pi@pilabs ~ $ chmod +x $HOME/bin/hello1.sh
pi@pilabs ~ $ hello1.sh
Hello World
pi@pilabs ~ $ _
```

Checking the exit status

This script is simple, but we still need to know how to make use of the exit codes from scripts and other applications. The command-line list that we generated earlier, while creating the `$HOME/bin` directory, is a good example of how we can use the exit code:

```
$ command1 || command 2
```

In the preceding example, command2 is executed only if command1 fails in some way. To be specific, command2 will run if command1 exits with a status code other than 0.

Similarly, in the following extract, we will only execute command2 if command1 succeeds and issues an exit code of 0:

```
$ command1 && command2
```

To read the exit code from our script explicitly, we can view the $? variable, as shown in the following example:

```
$ hello1.sh
$ echo $?
```

The expected output is 0, as this is what we have added to the last line of the file and there is precious little else that can go wrong to cause the failure to reach that line.

Ensuring a unique name

We can now create and execute a simple script, but we need to consider the name a little. In this case, hello1.sh will be good enough and is unlikely to clash with anything else on the system. We should avoid using names that may clash with existing aliases, functions, keywords, and building commands, as well as avoiding names of programs already in use.

Adding the sh suffix to the file does not guarantee the name will be unique, but, in Linux, where we do not use file extensions, the suffix is part of the filename. This helps you to provide a unique identity to your script. Additionally, the suffix is used by the editor to help you identify the file for syntax highlighting. If you recall, we specifically added the syntax highlighting file sh.nanorc to the nano text editor. Each of these files is specific to a suffix and subsequent language.

Referring back to the command hierarchy within this chapter, we can use a type to determine the location and type of file hello.sh:

```
$ type hello1.sh  #To determine the type and path
$ type -a hello1.sh  #To print all commands found if the name is NOT unique
$ type -t hello1.sh ~To print the simple type of the command
```

These commands and output can be seen in the following screenshot:

```
pi@pilabs ~ $ type hello1.sh
hello1.sh is hashed (/home/pi/bin/hello1.sh)
pi@pilabs ~ $ type -a hello1.sh
hello1.sh is /home/pi/bin/hello1.sh
pi@pilabs ~ $ type -t hello1.sh
file
pi@pilabs ~ $ _
```

Hello Dolly!

It is possible that we might need a little more substance in the script than a simple fixed message. Static message content does have its place, but we can make this script much more useful by building in some flexibility.

In this chapter, we will look at the positional parameters or arguments that we can supply to the script and in the next chapter, we will see how we can make the script interactive and also prompt the user for input at runtime.

Running the script with arguments

We can run the script with arguments; after all, it's a free world and Linux promotes your freedom to do what you want to do with the code. However, if the script does not make use of the arguments, then they will be silently ignored. The following command shows the script running with a single argument:

```
$ hello1.sh fred
```

The script will still run and will not produce an error. The output will not change either and will print Hello World:

Argument Identifier	Description
$0	The name of the script itself, which is often used in usage statements.
$1	A positional argument, which is the first argument passed to the script.
${10}	Where two or more digits are needed to represent the argument position. Brace brackets are used to delimit the variable name from any other content. Single value digits are expected.
$#	The argument count is especially useful when we need to set the amount of arguments needed for correct script execution.
$*	Refers to all arguments.

For the script to make use of the argument, we can change its content a little. Let's first copy the script, add in the execute permissions, and then edit the new hello2.sh:

```
$ cp $HOME/bin/hello1.sh $HOME/bin/hello2.sh
$ chmod +x $HOME/bin/hello2.sh
```

We need to edit the hello2.sh file to make use of the argument as it is passed at the command line. The following screenshot shows the simplest use of command-line arguments, now allowing us to have a custom message:

```
#!/bin/bash
echo "Hello $1"
exit 0
~
```

Run the script now; we can provide an argument as shown in the following:

```
$ hello2.sh fred
```

The output should now say `Hello fred`. If we do not provide an argument, then the variable will be empty and will just print `Hello`. You can refer to the following screenshot to see the execution argument and output:

```
pi@pilabs ~ $ hello2.sh fred
Hello fred
pi@pilabs ~ $ _
```

If we adjust the script to use `$*`, all the arguments will print. We will see `Hello` and then a list of all the supplied arguments. Edit the script and replace the `echo` line as follows:

```
echo "Hello $*"
```

This will execute the script with the following arguments:

```
$ hello2.sh fred wilma betty barney
```

And this will result in the output shown in the following screenshot:

```
pi@pilabs ~ $
pi@pilabs ~ $ hello2.sh fred wilma betty barney
Hello fred wilma betty barney
pi@pilabs ~ $ _
```

If we want to print `Hello <name>`, with each name on a separate line, we will need to wait a little until we cover looping structures. A `for` loop is a good way to achieve this.

The importance of correct quotes

So far, we have used a simple double-quoting mechanism to encase the strings that we want to use with echo.

In the first script, it does not matter if we use single or double quotes. `echo "Hello World"` will be exactly the same as `echo 'Hello World'`.

However, this is not the case in the second script, so it is very important to understand the quoting mechanisms available in bash.

As we have seen, using double quotes in `echo "Hello $1"` will result in `Hello fred` or whatever the supplied value is. Whereas, if we use single quotes in `echo 'Hello $1'`, the printed output on the screen will be `Hello $1`; that is, we see the variable name and not its value.

The idea of the quotes is to protect special characters, such as a space between the two words; both quotes protect the space from being misinterpreted. The space is normally read as a default field, separated by the shell. In other words, all characters are read by the shell as literals with no special meaning. This has the knock-on effect of the `$` symbol printing its literal format rather than allowing bash to expand its value. The bash shell is prevented from expanding the variable's value as it is protected by the single quotes.

This is where the double quote comes to our rescue. The double quote will protect all the characters except the `$`, allowing bash to expand the stored value.

If we ever need to use a literal `$` within the quoted string, along with variables that need to be expanded, we can use double quotes, but escape the desired `$` with the backslash (\). For example, `echo "$USER earns \$4"` would print as `Fred earns $4` if the current user were Fred.

Try the following examples at the command line using all quoting mechanisms. Feel free to up your hourly rate as required:

```
$ echo "$USER earns $4"
$ echo '$USER earns $4'
$ echo "$USER earns \$4"
```

The output is shown in the following screenshot:

```
pi@pilabs ~ $ echo "$USER earns $4"
pi earns
pi@pilabs ~ $ echo '$USER earns $4'
$USER earns $4
pi@pilabs ~ $ echo "$USER earns \$4"
pi earns $4
pi@pilabs ~ $ _
```

Printing the script name

The $0 variable represents the script name, and this is often used in usage statements. As we are not yet looking at conditional statements, we will get the script name printed above the displayed name.

Edit your script so that it reads like the following complete code block for $HOME/bin/hello2.sh:

```
#!/bin/bash
echo "You are using $0"
echo "Hello $*"
exit 0
```

The output from the command is shown in the following screenshot:

```
pi@pilabs ~ $ hello2.sh fred
You are using /home/pi/bin/hello2.sh
Hello fred
pi@pilabs ~ $
```

If we prefer not to print the path and only want the name of the script to show, we can use the basename command, which extracts the name from the path. Adjust the script so that the second line now reads as follows:

```
echo "You are using $(basename $0)"
```

The $(....) syntax is used to evaluate the output of the inner command. We first run basename $0 and feed the result into an unnamed variable represented by the $.

The new output will appear as seen in the following screenshot:

```
pi@pilabs ~ $ hello2.sh fred
You are using hello2.sh
Hello fred
```

It is possible to achieve the same results using back quotes; this is less easy to read, but we have mentioned this as you might need to understand and modify the scripts that have been written by others. The alternative to the $(....) syntax is shown in the following example:

```
echo "You are using 'basename $0'"
```

Please note that the characters used are back quotes and *NOT* single quotes. On UK and US keyboards, these are found in the top-left corner next to the number 1 key.

Declaring variables

Just like in any programming language, you can declare variables in bash scripts. So, what are these variables and what are the benefits of using them?

Well, a variable is like a placeholder where you store some value for later use in your code.

There are two kinds of variables you can declare in your script:

- User-defined variables
- Environment variables

User-defined variables

To declare a variable, just type the name you want and set its value using the equals sign (=).

Check out this example:

```
#!/bin/bash
name="Mokhtar"
age=35
total=16.5
echo $name   #prints Mokhtar
echo $age    #prints 35
echo $total  #prints 16.5
```

As you can see, to print the variable's value, you should use the dollar sign ($) before it.

Note that there are **no spaces** between the variable name and the equals sign, or between the equals sign and the value.

If you forget and type a space in between, the shell will treat the variable as if it were a command, and, since there is no such command, it will show an error.

All of the following examples are incorrect declarations:

```
# Don't declare variables like this:
name = "Mokhtar"
age =35
total= 16.5
```

Another useful type of user-defined variable is the array. An array can hold multiple values. So, if you have tens of values you want to use, you should use arrays instead of filling your script with variables.

To declare an array, just enclose its elements between brackets, like this:

```
#!/bin/bash
myarr=(one two three four five)
```

To access a specific array element, you can specify its index like this:

```
#!/bin/bash
myarr=(one two three four five)
echo ${myarr[1]} #prints two which is the second element
```

The index is zero based.

To print the array elements, you can use an asterisk, like this:

```
#!/bin/bash
myarr=(one two three four five)
echo ${myarr[*]}
```

To remove a specific element from the array, you can use the `unset` command:

```
#!/bin/bash
myarr=(one two three four five)
unset myarr[1]  #This will remove the second element
unset myarr     #This will remove all elements
```

Environment variables

So far, we have used variables that we didn't define, such as $BASH_VERSION, $HOME, $PATH, and $USER. You might wonder, as we didn't declare these variables, where did they come from?

These variables are defined by the shell for your use and they are called environment variables.

There are many environment variables. If you want to list them, you can use the `printenv` command.

Also, you can print a specific environment variable by specifying it to the `printenv` command:

```
$ printenv HOME
```

We can use any of these variables in our bash scripts.

Note that all environment variables are written in capital letters, so you can declare your variables as lower case to make it easy to differentiate your variables from environment variables. This is not required, but is preferable.

Variable scope

Once you have declared your variable, it will be available for use in your entire bash script without any problems.

Let's assume this scenario: you have divided your code into two files and you will execute one of them from inside the other, like this:

```
# The first script
#!/bin/bash
name="Mokhtar"
./script2.sh # This will run the second script
```

The second script looks like this:

```
# The script2.sh script
#!/bin/bash
echo $name
```

Suppose that you want to use the `name` variable in the second script. If you try to print it, nothing will show up; this is because a variable's scope is only limited to the process that creates it.

To use the `name` variable, you can export it using the `export` command.

So, our code will be like this:

```
# The first script
#!/bin/bash
name="Mokhtar"
export name # The variable will be accessible to other processes
./script2.sh
```

Now if you run the first script, it will print the name that came from the first script file.

Keep in mind that the second process or `script2.sh` only makes a copy of the variable and never touches the original one.

To prove this, try to change that variable from the second script and try to access that variable value from the first script:

```
# The first script
#!/bin/bash
name="Mokhtar"
export name
./script2.sh
echo $name
```

The second script will be like this:

```
# The first script
#!/bin/bash
name="Another name"
echo $name
```

If you run the first script, it will print the modified name from the second script and then it will print the original name from the first script. So, the original variable remains as it is.

Command substitution

So far, we have seen how to declare variables. These variables can hold integers, strings, arrays, or floats, as we have seen, but this is not everything.

A command substitution means storing the output of a command execution in a variable.

As you might know, the `pwd` command prints the current working directory. So, we will see how to store its value in a variable.

There are two ways to perform a command substitution:

- Using the backtick character (`'`)
- Using the dollar sign format, like this: `$()`

Using the first method, we just surround the command between two backticks:

```
#!/bin/bash
cur_dir='pwd'
echo $cur_dir
```

And the second way is written as follows:

```
#!/bin/bash
cur_dir=$(pwd)
echo $cur_dir
```

The output coming from commands can be further processed and actions can be made based on that output.

Debugging your scripts

With the scripts as simple as we have seen so far, there is little that can go wrong or need debugging. As the script grows and decision paths are included with conditional statements, we may need to use some level of debugging to analyze the scripts' progress better.

Bash provides two options for us, `-v` and `-x`.

If we want to look at the verbose output from our script and the detailed information about the way the script is evaluated line by line, we can use the `-v` option. This can be within the shebang, but it is often easier to run the script directly with bash:

```
$ bash -v $HOME/bin/hello2.sh fred
```

This is especially useful in this example as we can see how each element of the embedded `basename` command is processed. The first step is removing the quotes and then the parentheses. Take a look at the following output:

```
pi@pilabs ~ $ bash -v $HOME/bin/hello2.sh fred
#!/bin/bash
echo "You are using $(basename $0)"
basename $0)"
basename $0)
basename $0
You are using hello2.sh
echo "Hello $*"
Hello fred
exit 0
pi@pilabs ~ $ _
```

The `-x` option, which displays the commands as they are executed, is more commonly used. It's useful to know the decision branch that has been chosen by the script. The following shows this in action:

```
$ bash -x $HOME/bin/hello2.sh fred
```

We again see that the `basename` is evaluated first, but we do not see the more detailed steps involved in running that command. The screenshot that follows captures the command and output:

```
pi@pilabs ~ $ bash -x $HOME/bin/hello2.sh fred
++ basename /home/pi/bin/hello2.sh
+ echo 'You are using hello2.sh'
You are using hello2.sh
+ echo 'Hello fred'
Hello fred
+ exit 0
pi@pilabs ~ $ _
```

The previous method might be hard for beginners or people who have a programming background in which they debugged their code visually.

Another modern way of debugging shell scripts is by using Visual Studio Code.

There is a plugin called **bash debug** that enables you to debug bash scripts visually, as is the case for any other programming language.

You can step into, step over, add watches, and do all the other usual debugging stuff you know.

After installing the plugin, from the **File** menu, open your shell-scripts folder. Then you can configure the debugging process by pressing *Ctrl + Shift + P* and typing the following:

```
Debug:open launch.json
```

This will open an empty file; type in the following configurations:

```
{
    "version": "0.2.0",
    "configurations": [
        {
            "name": "Packt Bash-Debug",
            "type": "bashdb",
            "request": "launch",
            "scriptPath": "${command:SelectScriptName}",
            "commandLineArguments": "",
            "linux": {
                "bashPath": "bash"
            },
            "osx": {
                "bashPath": "bash"
            }
        }
    ]
}
```

This will create a debug configuration named `Packt Bash-Debug`:

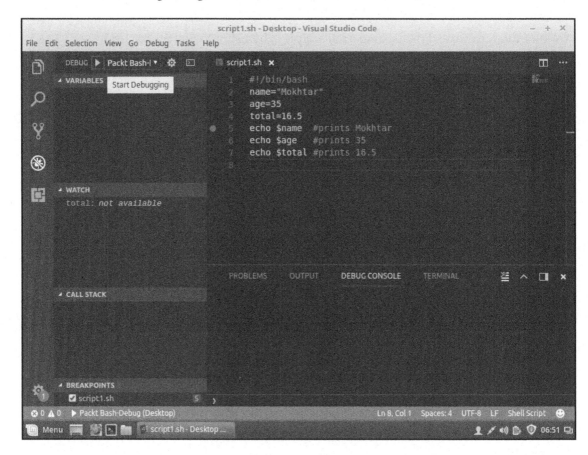

Now insert a breakpoint and press *F5*, or start debugging from the **Debug** menu; it will show you the list of .sh files:

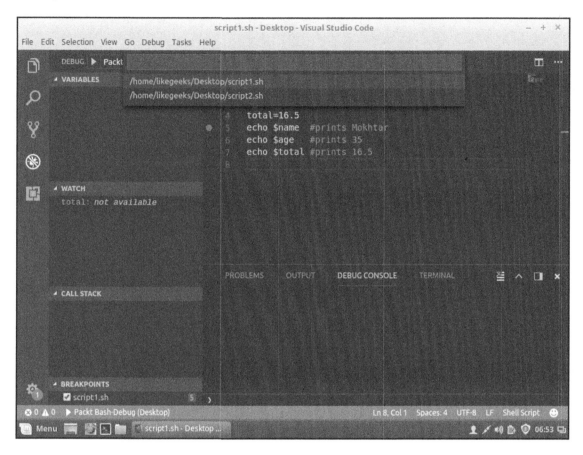

Select the one you want to debug, and set a breakpoint on any line to test it, as shown in the following screenshot:

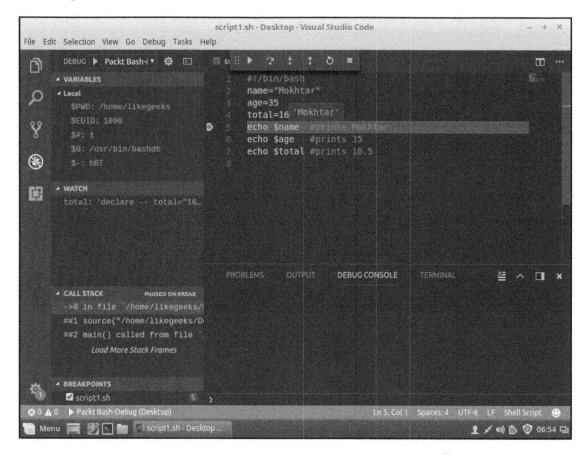

You can add watches to watch variables' values while stepping over your lines of code:

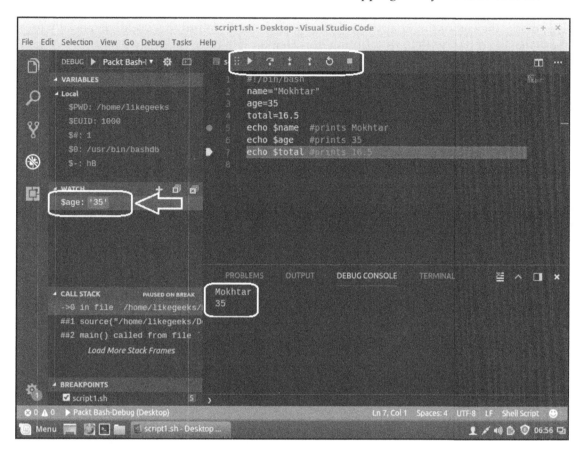

 Note that your script **MUST** start with the bash shebang, `#!/bin/bash`.

Now you can enjoy the visual method of debugging. Happy coding!

Summary

This marks the end of this chapter and you have no doubt found this useful. Especially for those making a start with bash scripting, this chapter will have established a firm foundation on which you can build your knowledge.

We began by ensuring that bash is secure and not susceptible to shell-shock from embedded functions. With bash secured, we considered the execution hierarchy where aliases, functions, and so on are checked before the command; knowing this can help us plan a good naming structure and a path to locate the scripts.

Then we went on to illustrate the types of Linux shells and we found out what bash scripting is.

Soon, we were writing simple scripts with static content, but we saw how easy it was to add flexibility using arguments. The exit code from the script can be read with the $? variable and we can create a command-line list using || and &&, which depends on the success or failure of the preceding command in the list.

Then we saw how to declare variables and how to use environment variables. We identified the variables' scope and saw how to export them to another process.

Also, we saw how to store commands' output in variables, which is called command substitution.

Finally, we closed the chapter by looking at debugging the script using bash options and VS Code. It's not really required when the script is trivial, but it will be useful later when complexity is added.

In the next chapter, we will create interactive scripts that read the user's input during script execution.

Questions

1. What is the problem with the following code? And how do we fix it?

```
#!/bin/bash
var1 ="Welcome to bash scripting ..."
echo $var1
```

2. What is the result of the following code?

```
#!/bin/bash
arr1=(Saturday Sunday Monday Tuesday Wednesday)
echo ${arr1[3]}
```

3. What is the problem with the following code? And how do we fix it?

```
#!/bin/bash
files = 'ls -la'
echo $files
```

4. What is the value of the b and c variables in the following code?

```
#!/bin/bash
a=15
b=20
c=a
b=c
```

Further reading

Please see the following for further reading relating to this chapter:

- http://tldp.org/HOWTO/Bash-Prog-Intro-HOWTO-5.html
- http://tldp.org/LDP/abs/html/varassignment.html
- http://tldp.org/LDP/abs/html/declareref.html

2
Creating Interactive Scripts

In `Chapter 1`, *The What and Why of Scripting with Bash*, we learned how to create a script and use some of its basic elements. These included optional parameters that we can pass through to the script when it is executed. In this chapter, we will extend this by using the shell's built-in `read` command to allow for interactive scripts. Interactive scripts are scripts that prompt for information during the script's execution.

In this chapter, we will cover the following topics:

- Using `echo` with options
- Basic script using `read`
- Script comments
- Enhancing read scripts with `read` prompts
- Limiting the number of entered characters
- Controlling the visibility of the entered text
- Passing options
- Read options values
- Try to be standard
- Enhancing learning with simple scripts

Technical requirements

The source code for this chapter can be downloaded from here:

```
https://github.com/PacktPublishing/Mastering-Linux-Shell-Scripting-Second-
Edition/tree/master/Chapter02
```

Using echo with options

So far, in this book we have been able to see that the echo command is very useful and is going to be used in many of our scripts, if not all of them. When running the echo command, the built-in command will be used unless we state the full path to the file. We can test this with the following command:

```
$ which echo
```

To gain help on the built-in command, we can use man bash and search for echo; however, the echo command is identical to the internal command, so we recommend that you use man echo in most cases in order to display the command options.

The basic use of echo that we have seen so far will produce a text output and a new line. This is often the desired response, so we don't need to be concerned that the next prompt will append to the end of the echoed text. The new line separates the script output from the next shell prompt. If we do not supply any text string to print, echo will print only the new line to STDOUT. We can test this with the following command, directly from the command line. We do not need to run echo or, in fact, any other command from a script. To run echo from the command line, we simply enter the command as shown:

```
$ echo
```

The output will show a clear new line between the command we issued and the subsequent prompt. We can see this in the following screenshot:

```
pi@pilabs ~ $ echo

pi@pilabs ~ $ _
```

If we want to suppress the new line, which is especially useful if we are to prompt users, we can do this in the following two ways, with the help of echo:

```
$ echo -n "Which directory do you want to use? "
$ echo -e "Which directory do you want to use? \c"
```

The result will be to suppress the line feed. In the initial example, the −n option is used to suppress the line feed. The second example uses the more generic −e option, which allows escape sequences to be added to the text string. To continue on the same line, we use \c as the escape sequence.

This does not look great as the final part of the script or when it is run from the command line, as the command prompt will follow. This is illustrated in the following screenshot:

```
pi@pilabs ~ $ echo -e "Which directory do you want to use? \c"
Which directory do you want to use? pi@pilabs ~ $ _
```

Basic script using read

When used as part of a script that prompts for user input, the suppression of the line feed is exactly what we want. We will begin by copying the existing hello2.sh script to hello3.sh and build an interactive script. Initially, we will use echo as the prompt mechanism, but, as we gradually enhance the script, we will generate the prompt directly from the shell built-in read command:

```
$ cp $HOME/bin/hello2.sh $HOME/bin/hello3.sh
$ chmod +x $HOME/bin/hello3.sh
```

Edit the $HOME/bin/hello3.sh script so that it reads as follows:

```
#!/bin/bash
echo -n "Hello $(basename $0)! May I ask your name: "
read
echo "Hello $REPLY"
exit 0
```

As we execute the script, we will be greeted and prompted with whatever is typed. This is echoed using the $REPLY variable in the echo statement. As we have not yet supplied a variable name to the read built-in command, the default $REPLY variable is used. The script execution and output are shown in the following screenshot. Take some time to practice the script on your own system.

This little step has taken us a long way and there are many uses for a script like this; we have all used installation scripts that prompt for options and directories as we run through the install. We accept that it is still quite trivial, but, as we delve into the chapter, we will get closer to some more useful scripts.

Script comments

We should always introduce commenting scripts early in the piece. A script comment is prefaced with a # symbol. Anything after the # symbol is a comment and is not evaluated by the script. The shebang, `#!/bin/bash`, is primarily a comment and, as such, is not evaluated by the shell. The shell running the script reads the whole shebang, so it knows which command interpreter to hand the script over to. A comment may be at the start of a line or partway into the line. Shell scripting does not have the notion of multi-line comments.

If you are not already familiar with comments, then please note that they are added to the script to describe who wrote the script, when it was written and last updated, and what the script does. They are the metadata of the script.

The following is an example of comments in scripts:

```
#!/bin/bash
# Welcome to bash scripting
# Author: Mokhtar
# Date: 1/5/2018
```

It is good practice to comment, and add comments that explain what the code is doing and why. This will help you and your colleagues who need to edit the script at a later date.

Enhancing scripts with read prompts

We have seen how we can use the built-in read to populate a variable. So far, we have used echo to produce the prompt, but this can be passed to read itself using the –p option. The `read` command will surpass the additional linefeed, so we reduce both the line count and the complexity to some degree.

We can test this at the command line itself. Try typing the following command to see `read` in action:

```
$ read -p "Enter your name: " name
```

We use the `read` command with the `-p` option. The argument that follows the option is the text that appears in the prompt. Normally, we would make sure that there is a trailing space at the end of the text to ensure that we can clearly see what we type. The last argument supplied here is the variable we want to populate; we simply call it name. Variables are case-sensitive too. Even if we do not supply the last argument, we can still store the user's response, but this time in the `REPLY` variable.

When we return the value of a variable, we use $, but not when we write it. In simple terms, when reading a variable we refer to `$VAR` and when setting a variable we refer to `VAR=value`.

The `read` command with syntax using the `-p` option is shown as follows:

```
read -p <prompt> <variable name>
```

We can edit the script so that it appears similar to the following extract from `hello3.sh`:

```
#!/bin/bash
read -p "May I ask your name: " name
echo "Hello $name"
exit 0
```

The `read` prompt cannot evaluate commands within the message string, such as those we used before.

Limiting the number of entered characters

We have not needed this functionality in the scripts we have used so far, but we may need to ask users to hit any key to continue. At the moment, we have set it up in such a way that the variable is not populated until we hit the *Enter* key. Users have to hit *Enter* to continue. If we use the `-n` option followed by an integer, we can specify the number of characters to accept before continuing; we will set 1 in this case. Take a look at the following code extract:

```
#!/bin/bash
read -p "May I ask your name: " name
echo "Hello $name"
read -n1 -p "Press any key to exit"
echo
exit 0
```

Now the script will pause after displaying the name until we press any key; we can literally press any key before continuing, as we accept just 1 key stroke, whereas earlier we were required to leave the default behavior in place, as we could not know how long an entered name would be. We have to wait for the user to hit *Enter*.

 We add an additional echo here to ensure that a new line is issued before the script ends. This ensures that the shell prompt starts on a new line.

Controlling the visibility of the entered text

Even though we have limited the input to a single character, we do get to see the text on the screen. In the same way, if we type the name, we get to see the entered text before we hit *Enter*. In this case, it is just untidy, but if we are entering sensitive data, such as a PIN or a password, we should hide the text. We can use the silent option, or –s, to achieve this. A simple edit in the script will set this in place:

```
#!/bin/bash
read -p "May I ask your name: " name
echo "Hello $name"
read -sn1 -p "Press any key to exit"
echo
exit 0
```

Now, when we use a key to continue, it will not be displayed on the screen. We can see the behavior of the script in the following screenshot:

```
pi@pilabs ~ $ hello3.sh
May I ask your name: fred          We see the entered text
Hello fred
Press any key to continue    With -s we don't see the entered text
pi@pilabs ~ $ _
```

Passing options

So far, we have seen in the first chapter how to read parameters from the user. Also, you can pass options. So, what are options? And how are they different from parameters?

Options are characters with a single dash before them.

Check out this example:

```
$ ./script1.sh -a
```

The −a is an option. You can check from your script if the user entered this option; if so, then your script can behave in some manner.

You can pass multiple options:

```
$ ./script1.sh -a -b -c
```

To print these options, you can use the $1, $2, and $3 variables:

```
#!/bin/bash
echo $1
echo $2
echo $3
```

We should check these options, but, since we haven't discussed conditional statements yet, we will keep it simple for now.

Options can be passed with a value, like this:

```
$ ./script1.sh -a -b 20 -c
```

Here the −b option is passed with a value of 20.

As you can see, the variable $3=20, which is the passed value.

This might not be acceptable to you. You need $2=-b and $3=-c.

We will use some conditional statements to get these options correct.

```
#!/bin/bash
while [ -n "$1" ]
do
case "$1" in
-a) echo "-a option used" ;;
-b) echo "-b option used" ;;
-c) echo "-c option used" ;;
*) echo "Option $1 not an option" ;;
esac
shift
done
```

If you don't know about the while loop, it's not a problem; we will discuss conditional statements in detail in the coming chapters.

The shift command shifts the options one step to the left.

So, if we have three options or parameters and we use the shift command:

- $3 becomes $2
- $2 becomes $1
- $1 is dropped

It's like an action to move forward while iterating over the options using the while loop.

So, in the first loop cycle, $1 will be the first option. After shifting the options, $1 will be the second option and so on.

If you try the previous code, you will notice that it still doesn't identify the values of options correctly. Don't worry, the solution is coming; just wait a little longer.

Passing parameters with options

To pass parameters along with options simultaneously, you must separate them with a double dash, like this:

```
$ ./script1.sh -a -b -c -- p1 p2 p3
```

Using the previous technique, we can iterate over the options till we reach the double dash, then we will iterate over the parameters:

```
#!/bin/bash
while [ -n "$1" ]
do
case "$1" in
-a) echo "-a option found" ;;
-b) echo "-b option found";;
-c) echo "-c option found" ;;
--) shift
break ;;
*) echo "Option $1 not an option";;
esac
shift
done
#iteration over options is finished here.
#iteration over parameters started.
num=1
for param in $@
do
echo "#$num: $param"
num=$(( $num + 1 ))
done
```

Now if we run it with parameters and options combined, we should see a list of options and another list of parameters:

```
$ ./script1.sh -a -b -c -- p1 p2 p3
```

As you can see, anything passed after the double dash is treated as a parameter.

Read options values

We have seen how to identify options and parameters, but we still need a way to read the options values correctly.

You may need to pass a value for a specific option. How can this value be read?

We will check for the $2 variable while the iteration goes through the options that we expect a value for.

Check the following code:

```
#!/bin/bash
while [ -n "$1" ]
do
case "$1" in
-a) echo "-a option passed";;
-b) param="$2"
echo "-b option passed, with value $param"
shift ;;
-c) echo "-c option passed";;
--) shift
break ;;
*) echo "Option $1 not an option";;
esac
shift
done
num=1
for param in "$@"
do
echo "#$num: $param"
num=$(( $num + 1 ))
done
```

```
                    likegeeks@likegeeks-VirtualBox ~/Desktop
  File  Edit  View  Search  Terminal  Help
  likegeeks@likegeeks-VirtualBox ~/Desktop $ ./script1.sh -a -b 20 -c
  -a option passed
  -b option passed, with value 20
  -c option passed
  likegeeks@likegeeks-VirtualBox ~/Desktop $
```

This looks good now; your script identifies the options and the passed value for the second option.

There is a built-in option for getting options from the users, which is using the `getopt` function.

Unfortunately, `getopt` doesn't support options with more than one character.

There is a non-built-in program called `getopt`, which supports options larger than one character, but, again, the macOS X version doesn't support long options.

Anyway, if you would like to read more about `getopt` usage, refer to the further reading resources given after this chapter.

Try to be standard

You may use bash scripts from GitHub, and you may notice that there is a standard option scheme that is followed. It's not required, but it is preferable.

These are some of the commonly used options:

- `-a`: List all items
- `-c`: Get a count of all items
- `-d`: Output directory
- `-e`: Expand items
- `-f`: Specify a file
- `-h`: Show the help page
- `-i`: Ignore the character case
- `-l`: List a text
- `-o`: Send output to a file
- `-q`: Keep silent; don't ask the user
- `-r`: Process something recursively
- `-s`: Use stealth mode
- `-v`: Use verbose mode
- `-x`: Specify an executable
- `-y`: Accept without prompting me

Enhancing learning with simple scripts

Our scripts are still a little trivial, and we have not looked at conditional statements so we can test for correct input, but let's take a look at some simple scripts that we can build with some functionality.

Backing-up with scripts

Now that we have created some scripts, we may want to back these up to a different location. If we create a script to prompt us, we can choose the location and the type of files that we want to backup.

Consider the following script for your first practice. Create the script and name it $HOME/backup.sh:

```
#!/bin/bash
# Author: @theurbanpenguin
# Web: www.theurbapenguin.com
# Script to prompt to back up files and location
# The files will be search on from the user's home
# directory and can only be backed up to a directory
# within $HOME
# Last Edited: July 4 2015
read -p "Which file types do you want to backup " file_suffix
read -p "Which directory do you want to backup to " dir_name
# The next lines creates the directory if it does not exist
test -d $HOME/$dir_name || mkdir -m 700 $HOME/$dir_name
# The find command will copy files the match the
# search criteria ie .sh . The -path, -prune and -o
# options are to exclude the backdirectory from the
# backup.
find $HOME -path $HOME/$dir_name -prune -o \
-name "*$file_suffix" -exec cp {} $HOME/$dir_name/ \;
exit 0
```

You will see that the file is commented; though, in black and white, the readability is a little difficult. If you have an electronic copy of this book, you should see the colors in the following screenshot:

```bash
#!/bin/bash
# Author: @theurbanpenguin
# Web: www.theurbapenguin.com
# Script to prompt to back up files and location
# The files will be search on from the user's home
# directory and can only be backed up to a directory
# within $HOME
# Last Edited: July 4 2015
read -p "Which file types do you want to backup " file_suffix
read -p "Which directory do you want to backup to " dir_name
# The next lines creates the directory if it does not exist
test -d $HOME/$dir_name || mkdir -m 700 $HOME/$dir_name
# The find command will copy files the match the
# search criteria ie .sh . The -path, -prune and -o
# options are to exclude the backdirectory from the
# backup.
find $HOME -path $HOME/$dir_name -prune -o \
 -name "*$file_suffix" -exec cp {} $HOME/$dir_name/ \;
exit 0
```

As the script runs, you may choose .sh for the files to backup and backup as the directory. The script execution is shown in the following screenshot, along with a listing of the directory:

```
pi@pilabs ~ $ backup.sh
Which file types do you want to backup .sh
Which directory do you want to backup to backup
pi@pilabs ~ $ ls $HOME/backup
                                irix.sh


                                mksmime-certs.sh

CA.sh
                                profile.sh
                 hpux10-cc.sh
                                pthread.sh
pi@pilabs ~ $ _
```

Now you can see that we can start to create meaningful scripts with trivial scripting; although we strongly urge adding error checking of the user input if this script is for something other than personal use. As we progress into the book, we will cover this.

Connecting to a server

Let's look at some practical scripts that we can use to connect to servers. Firstly, we will look at ping, and in the second script we will look at prompting for SSH credentials.

Version 1 – ping

This is something we can all do, as no special services are required. This will simplify the ping command for console users who may not know the details of the command. This will ping the server for just three counts rather than the normal infinite amount. There is no output if the server is alive, but a failed server reports sever dead. Create the following script as $HOME/bin/ping_server.sh:

```
#!/bin/bash
# Author: @theurbanpenguin
# Web: www.theurbapenguin.com
# Script to ping a server
# Last Edited: July 4 2015
read -p "Which server should be pinged " server_addr
ping -c3 $server_addr 2>1 > /dev/null || echo "Server Dead"
```

The following screenshot shows successful and failed outputs:

```
pi@pilabs ~ $
pi@pilabs ~ $ ping_server.sh
Which server should be pinged localhost
pi@pilabs ~ $ ping_server.sh
Which server should be pinged 1.2.3.4
Server Dead
pi@pilabs ~ $ _
```

Version 2 – SSH

Often SSH is installed and running on servers, so you may be able to run this script if your system is running SSH or you have access to an SSH server. In this script, we prompt for the server address and username, and pass them through to the SSH client. Create the following script as $HOME/bin/connect_server.sh:

```
#!/bin/bash
# Author: @theurbanpenguin
# Web: www.theurbapenguin.com
```

```
# Script to prompt fossh connection
# Last Edited: July 4 2015
read -p "Which server do you want to connect to: " server_name
read -p "Which username do you want to use: " user_name
ssh ${user_name}@$server_name
```

 Use of the brace bracket is to delimit the variable from the @ symbol in the last line of the script.

Version 3 – MySQL/MariaDB

In the next script, we will provide the detail for a database connection along with the SQL query to execute. You will be able to run this if you have a MariaDB or MySQL database server on your system, or one that you can connect to. For this demonstration, we will use Linux Mint 18.3 and MariaDB version 10; however, this should work for any MySQL server or MariaDB, from version 5 onwards. The script collects user and password information as well as the SQL command to execute. Create the following script as $HOME/bin/run_mysql.sh:

```
#!/bin/bash
# Author: @theurbanpenguin
# Web: www.theurbapenguin.com
# Script to prompt for MYSQL user password and command
# Last Edited: July 4 2015
read -p "MySQL User: " user_name
read -sp "MySQL Password: " mysql_pwd
echo
read -p "MySQL Command: " mysql_cmd
read -p "MySQL Database: " mysql_db
mysql -u"$user_name" -p$mysql_pwd $mysql_db -Be"$mysql_cmd"
```

In this script, we can see that we suppress the display of the MySQL password when we input it into the read command using the -s option. Again, we use echo directly to ensure that the next prompt starts on a new line.

The script input is shown in the following screenshot:

```
andrew@web:~$ ./run_mysql.sh
MySQL User: andrew
MySQL Password:
MySQL Command: SHOW TABLES;
MySQL DB: wordpress
Tables_in_wordpress
wp_cleanup_optimizer_block_range_ip
wp_cleanup_optimizer_block_single_ip
wp_cleanup_optimizer_db_scheduler
wp_cleanup_optimizer_licensing
wp_cleanup_optimizer_login_log
wp_cleanup_optimizer_plugin_settings
wp_cleanup_optimizer_wp_scheduler
```

Now we can easily see the password suppression working and the ease of adding to the MySQL commands.

Reading files

The read command is not only used to read inputs from the user; you can use the read command to read files for further processing.

```
#!/bin/bash
while read line
do
echo $line
done < yourfile.txt
```

We redirect the file content to the while command to read the content using the read command, line by line.

Finally, we print the line using the echo command.

Summary

Feel proud that you now have your *I can read* badge for shell scripting. We have developed our scripts to be interactive and to prompt users for input during the script execution. These prompts can be used to simplify user operations on the command line. In this way, they do not need to remember the command-line options or have passwords that end up stored in the command-line history. When using passwords, we can simply store the value using the read -sp options.

Also, we saw how to pass options with and without values, and how to identify values correctly. We saw how to pass options and parameters at the same time, thanks to the double dash.

In the next chapter, we will take our time to look at the conditional statements in bash.

Questions

1. How many comments are in the following code?

   ```
   #!/bin/bash
   # Welcome to shell scripting
   # Author: Mokhtar
   ```

2. If we have the following code:

   ```
   #!/bin/bash
   echo $1
   echo $2
   echo $3
   ```

   And we run the script with these options:

   ```
   $ ./script1.sh -a -b50 -c
   ```

   What is the result of running this code?

3. Check the following code:

```
#!/bin/bash
shift
echo $#
```

If we run it with these options:

```
$ ./script1.sh Mokhtar -n -a 35 -p
```

1. What is the result?
2. What is the dropped parameter?

Further reading

Please see the following for further reading relating to this chapter:

- http://tldp.org/LDP/Bash-Beginners-Guide/html/sect_08_02.html
- https://ss64.com/bash/read.html
- http://www.manpagez.com/man/1/getopt/
- https://ss64.com/bash/getopts.html

Conditions Attached 3

Now you can make your scripts more interactive using the `read` command, and you know how to read parameters and options to lighten your inputs.

We can say that we are now into the fine print of the script. These are the details that are written into our scripts using conditions to test if a statement should run or not. We are now ready to add some intelligence into our scripts, so our scripts become more robust, easier to use, and more reliable. Conditional statements can be written with simple command-line lists of AND or OR commands together, or, more often, within traditional `if` statements.

In this chapter, we will cover the following topics:

- Simple decision paths using command-line lists
- Verifying user input with lists
- Using the test shell built-in
- Creating conditional statements using `if`
- Extending `if` with `else`
- Using the `test` command with the `if` command
- More conditions with `elif`
- Using case statements
- Recipe-frontend with `grep`

Technical requirements

The source code for this chapter can be downloaded from here:

```
https://github.com/PacktPublishing/Mastering-Linux-Shell-Scripting-Second-
Edition/tree/master/Chapter03
```

Simple decision paths using command-line lists

We have used command-line lists (|| and &&), both in Chapter 1, *The What and Why of Scripting with Bash*, and in some of the scripts found in Chapter 2, *Creating Interactive Scripts*. Lists are one of the simplest conditional statements that we can create, and so we thought that it was appropriate to use them in the earlier examples before fully explaining them here.

Command-line lists are two or more statements that are joined using either the AND or OR notations:

- &&: AND
- ||: OR

Where the two statements are joined using the AND notation, the second command only runs if the first command succeeds. Whereas, with the OR notation, the second command will run only if the first command fails.

The decision on the success or failure of a command is taken by reading the exit code from the application. A zero represents a successful application completion and anything other than a zero represents a failure. We can test the success or failure of an application by reading the exit status by means of the system variables $?. This is shown in the following example:

```
$ echo $?
```

If we need to ensure that a script is run from a user's home directory, we can build this into the script's logic. This can be tested from the command line, and it does not have to be in a script. Consider the following command-line example:

```
$ test $PWD == $HOME || cd $HOME
```

The double vertical bars denote an OR Boolean. This ensures that the second statement is only executed when the first statement is not true. In simple terms, if we are not currently in the home directory, we will be by the end of the command-line list. We will see more on the test command soon.

We can build this into almost any command that we want and not just test. For example, we can query to see if a user is logged into the system, and if they are, then we can use the write command to directly message their console. Similar to before, we can test this in the command line prior to adding it to the script. This is shown in the following command-line example:

```
$ who | grep pi > /dev/null 2>&1 && write pi < message.txt
```

Note that you should change the user pi to your username.

If we use this in a script, it is almost certain that we will replace the username with a variable. In general, if we need to refer to the same value more than once, then using a variable is a good idea. In this case, we are searching for the pi user.

When we break the command-line list down, we first use the who command to list the users who are logged on. We pipe the list to grep to search for the desired username. We are not interested in the output from the search, just its success or failure. Bearing this in mind, we redirect all our output to /dev/null. The double ampersand indicates that the second statement in the list runs only if the first returns true. If the pi user is logged on, we use write to message the user. The following screenshot illustrates this command and the output:

```
 pi@pilabs: ~
pi@pilabs ~ $ who | grep pi > /dev/null 2>&1 && write pi < message.txt

Message from pi@pilabs.theurbanpenguin.com on pts/0 at 10:42 ...
I see you are logged on then!

EOF
pi@pilabs ~ $ _
```

Verifying user input with lists

In this script, we will ensure that a value has been supplied to the first positional parameter. We can modify the hello2.sh script that we created in Chapter 1, *The What and Why of Scripting with Bash*, to check for user input before displaying the hello text.

You can copy the hello2.sh script to hello4.sh, or simply create a new script from scratch. There will not be a lot of typing and the script will be created as $HOME/bin/hello4.sh, as shown:

```
#!/bin/bash
echo "You are using $(basename $0)"
test -z $1 || echo "Hello $1"
exit 0
~
```

We can ensure that the script is executable by using the following command:

```
$ chmod +x $HOME/bin/hello4.sh
```

We can then run the script with or without arguments. The test statement is looking for the $1 variable to be zero bytes. If it is, then we will not see the hello statement; otherwise, it will print the hello message. In simple terms, we will see the hello message if we supply a name.

The following screenshot shows the output that you will see when you do not supply a parameter to the script, followed by the supplied parameter:

```
pi@pilabs: ~/bin
pi@pilabs ~/bin $ hello4.sh
You are using hello4.sh
pi@pilabs ~/bin $ hello4.sh bob
You are using hello4.sh
Hello bob
pi@pilabs ~/bin $ _
```

Using the test shell built-in

It is probably time for us to pull over to the side of the scripting highway and look a little more at the command test. This is both a shell built-in and a file executable in its own right. Of course, we will have to hit the built-in command first, unless we specify the full path to the file.

When the `test` command is run without any expressions to evaluate, then the test will return false. So, if we run the `test` as shown in the following command, the exit status will be 1, even though no error output is shown:

```
$ test
```

The `test` command will always return either `True` or `False`, or 0 or 1, respectively. The basic syntax of `test` is as follows:

```
test EXPRESSION
```

Or, we can invert the `test` command with this:

```
test ! EXPRESSION
```

If we need to include multiple expressions, this can be done using AND or OR together, using the -a and -o options, respectively:

```
test EXPRESSION -a EXPRESSION
test EXPRESSION -o EXPRESSION
```

We can also write this as a shorthand version, replacing the `test` with square brackets to surround the expression, as shown in the following example:

```
[ EXPRESSION ]
```

Testing strings

We can test for the equality or inequality of two strings. For example, one of the ways to test the root user is using the following command:

```
test $USER = root
```

We could also write this using the square bracket notation:

```
[ $USER = root ]
```

Note that you must put a space between each bracket and the inner testing condition as previously shown.

Equally, we could test for a non-root account with the following two methods:

```
test ! $USER = root
[ ! $USER = root ]
```

We can also test for the zero values or non-zero values of strings. We saw this in an earlier example in this chapter.

To test if a string has a value, we can use the −n option. We can check to see if the current connection is made through SSH by checking for the existence of a variable in the user's environment. We do this by using test and square brackets in the following two examples:

```
test -n $SSH_TTY
[ -n $SSH_TTY ]
```

If this is true, then the connection is made with SSH; if it is false, then the connection is not through SSH.

As we saw earlier, testing for a zero string value is useful when deciding if a variable is set:

```
test -z $1
```

Or, more simply, we could use the following:

```
[ -z $1 ]
```

A true result for this query means that no input parameters have been supplied to the script.

Testing integers

As well as testing string values of bash scripts, we can test for integer values and whole numbers. Another way of testing the input of a script is to count the numbers of positional parameters and also test if the number is above 0:

```
test $# -gt 0
```

Or using the brackets, as follows:

```
[ $# -gt 0 ]
```

When in a relationship, the top positional parameters of the $# variable represent the number of parameters passed to the script.

There are many tests that can be done for numbers:

- number1 −eq number2: This checks if number1 is equal to number2
- number1 −ge number2: This checks if number1 is greater than or equal to number2.

- number1 -gt number2: This checks if number1 is greater than number2
- number1 -le number2: This checks if number1 is smaller than or equal to number2
- number1 -lt number2: This checks if number1 is smaller than number2
- number1 -ne number2: This checks if number1 is not equal to number2

Testing file types

While testing for values, we can test for the existence of a file or file type. For example, we may only want to delete a file if it is a symbolic link. We use this while compiling a kernel. The /usr/src/linux directory should be a symbolic link to the latest kernel source code. If we download a newer version before compiling the new kernel, we need to delete the existing link and create a new link. Just in case someone has created the /usr/src/linux directory, we can test if it has a link before removing it:

```
# [ -h /usr/src/linux ] &&rm /usr/src/linux
```

The -h option tests that the file has a link. Other options include the following:

- -d: This shows that it's a directory
- -e: This shows that the file exists in any form
- -x: This shows that the file is executable
- -f: This shows that the file is a regular file
- -r: This shows that the file is readable
- -p: This shows that the file is a named pipe
- -b: This shows that the file is a block device
- file1 -nt file2: This checks if file1 is newer than file2
- file1 -ot file2: This checks if file1 is older than file2
- -O file: This checks if the logged-in user is the owner of the file
- -c: This shows that the file is a character device

More options do exist, so delve into the main pages as you need to. We will use different options throughout the book, and thus giving you practical and useful examples.

Creating conditional statements using if

As we have seen so far, it is possible to build simple conditions using command-line lists. These conditional statements can be written both with and without a test. As the complexity of the tasks increases, it becomes easier to create statements using if. This will certainly ease both the readability of the script and the logic layout. To a degree, it also matches the way in which we think and speak; if is a semantic in our spoken language in the same way it is within the bash script.

Even though it will take up more than a single line in the script, with an if statement we can achieve more and make the script more legible. That being said, let's look at creating if conditions. The following is an example of a script using an if statement:

```
#!/bin/bash
# Welcome script to display a message to users on login
# Author: @theurbanpenguin
# Date: 1/1/1971
if [ $# -lt 1 ] ; then
echo "Usage: $0 <name>"
exit 1
fi
echo "Hello $1"
exit 0
```

The code within the if statement will run only when the condition evaluates to true, and the end of the if block is denoted with fi - if backward. The color coding in vim can be useful to aid readability, which you will see in the following screenshot:

```
#!/bin/bash
# Welcome script to display a message to users on login
# Author: @theurbanpenguin
# Date: 1/1/1971
if [ $# -lt 1 ] ; then
  echo "Usage: $0 <name>"
  exit 1
fi
echo "Hello $1"
exit 0
```

Within the script, we can easily add in multiple statements to run when the condition is true. In our case, this includes exiting the script with an error indicated, as well as including the usage statement to assist the user. This ensures that we only display the hello message if we have supplied a name of the person to be welcomed.

We can view the script execution both with and without the argument in the following screenshot:

```
pi@pilabs ~ $ hello5.sh
Usage: /home/pi/bin/hello5.sh <name>
pi@pilabs ~ $ hello5.sh  fred
Hello fred
pi@pilabs ~ $ _
```

The following pseudocode shows the syntax of the `if` conditional statement:

```
if condition; then
    statement 1
    statement 2
fi
```

Indenting the code is not required, but it helps readability and is highly recommended. Adding the `then` statement to the same line as the `if` statement, again assists with the readability of the code, and the semicolon is required to separate the `if` from the `then`.

Extending if with else

When a script is required to continue regardless of the result of the `if` condition, it is often necessary to deal with both conditions of the evaluation, what to do when it is `true` as well as `false`. This is where we can make use of the `else` keyword. This allows the execution of one block of code when the condition is true and another when the condition is evaluated as false. The pseudocode for this is shown as follows:

```
if condition; then
    statement
else
    statement
fi
```

If we consider extending the `hello5.sh` script that we created earlier, it is easily possible to allow for the correct execution, regardless of the parameter being present or not. We can recreate this as `hello6.sh`, as follows:

```
#!/bin/bash
# Welcome script to display a message to users
# Author: @theurbanpenguin
# Date: 1/1/1971
if [ $# -lt 1 ] ; then
```

```
read -p "Enter a name: "
name=$REPLY
else
name=$1
fi
echo "Hello $name"
exit 0
```

The script now sets a named variable, which helps readability, and we can assign the correct value to $name from the input parameter or from the read prompt; either way the script is working well and starting to take shape.

Test command with the if command

You have seen how to use the test command or the short version [ ]. This test returns zero (true) or non-zero (false).

You will see how to check the returned result using the if command.

Checking strings

You can use the if command with the test command to check if the string matches a specific criterion:

- if [$string1 = $string2]: This checks if string1 is identical to string2
- if [$string1 != $string2]: This checks if string1 is not identical to string2
- if [$string1 \< $string2]: This checks if string1 is less than string2
- if [$string1 \> $string2]: This checks if string1 is greater than string2

The less than and greater than should be escaped with a backslash as if it shows a warning.

- if [-n $string1]: This checks if string1 is longer than zero
- if [-z $string1]: This checks if string1 has zero length

Let's see some examples to explain how if statements work:

```
#!/bin/bash
if [ "mokhtar" = "Mokhtar" ]
then
echo "Strings are identical"
```

```
else
echo "Strings are not identical"
fi
```

```
                    likegeeks@likegeeks-VirtualBox ~/Desktop        —  +  ×
  File  Edit  View  Search  Terminal  Help
  likegeeks@likegeeks-VirtualBox ~/Desktop $ ./script1.sh
  Strings are not idetical
  likegeeks@likegeeks-VirtualBox ~/Desktop $ █
```

This `if` statement checks if strings are identical or not; since the strings are not identical, because one of them has a capital letter, they are identified as not identical.

 Note the space between the square brackets and the variables; without this space it will show a warning in some cases.

The not-equal operator (`!=`) works the same way. Also, you can negate the `if` statement and it will work the same way, like this:

```
if ! [ "mokhtar" = "Mokhtar" ]
```

The less-than and greater-than operators check if the first string is greater than or less than the second string from the ASCII-order perspective:

```
#!/bin/bash
if [ "mokhtar" \> "Mokhtar" ]
then
echo "String1 is greater than string2"
else
echo "String1 is less than the string2"
fi
```

```
                    likegeeks@likegeeks-VirtualBox ~/Desktop        —  +  ×
  File  Edit  View  Search  Terminal  Help
  likegeeks@likegeeks-VirtualBox ~/Desktop $ ./script1.sh
  String1 is greater than string2
  likegeeks@likegeeks-VirtualBox ~/Desktop $ █
```

In the ASCII order, the lower-case characters are higher than the upper case.

Don't get confused if you use the `sort` command to sort a file or similar, and find that the sorting order works the opposite way to the `test` command. This is because the `sort` command uses the numbering order from the system settings, which is the opposite to the ASCII order.

To check the string length, you can use the `-n` test:

```
#!/bin/bash
if [ -n "mokhtar" ]
then
echo "String length is greater than zero"
else
echo "String is zero length"
fi
```

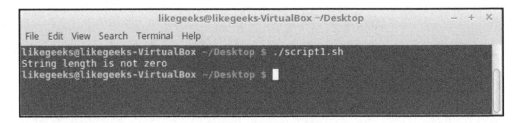

To check for a length of zero, you can use the `-z` test:

```
#!/bin/bash
if [ -z "mokhtar" ]
then
echo "String length is zero"
else
echo "String length is not zero"
fi
```

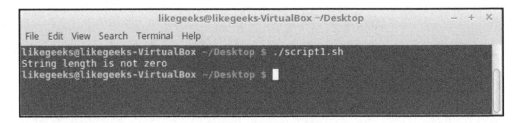

We have used quotes around the tested strings, even though our string has no spaces.

In case you have a string with spaces, you **MUST** use quotes.

Checking files and directories

Similarly, you can check files and directories using the `if` statement.

Let's look at an example:

```
#!/bin/bash
mydir=/home/mydir
if [ -d $mydir ]
then
echo "Directory $mydir exists."
else
echo "Directory $mydir not found."
fi
```

We used the `-d` test to check if the path is a directory.

The rest of the tests work the same way.

Checking numbers

Also, in the same way, we can check numbers using the `test` and the `if` commands.

```
#!/bin/bash
if [ 12 -gt 10 ]
then
echo "number1 is greater than number2"
else
echo "number1 is less than number2"
fi
```

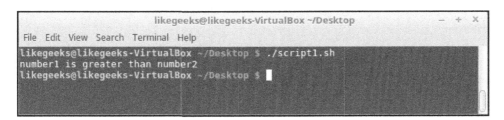

As expected, `12` is greater than `10`.

All other numeric tests work the same way.

Combining tests

You can combine multiple tests and check them using one `if` statement.

This is done using the AND (`&&`) and OR (`||`) commands:

```
#!/bin/bash
mydir=/home/mydir
name="mokhtar"
if [ -d $mydir ] && [ -n $name ]; then
    echo "The name is not zero length and the directory exists."
else
echo "One of the tests failed."
fi
```

The `if` statement performs two checks, it checks if the directory exists and that the name is not of zero length.

The two tests must return success (zero) to evaluate the next `echo` command.

If one of them fails, the `if` statement goes to the `else` clause.

Unlike the OR (`||`) command, if any of the tests returns success (zero), the `if` statement succeeds.

```
#!/bin/bash
mydir=/home/mydir
name="mokhtar"
if [ -d $mydir ] || [ -n $name ]; then
    echo "One of tests or both successes"
else
echo "Both failed"
fi
```

It is clear enough that if one of the tests returns true, the `if` statement returns true for the combined tests.

More conditions with elif

Moving on to where we require a greater degree of control, we can use the `elif` keyword. Unlike `else`, `elif` requires an additional condition to be tested for each `elif`. In this way, we can provide for different circumstances. We can add in as many `elif` conditions as required. The following shows some pseudocode:

```
if condition; then
statement
elif condition; then
statement
else
statement
fi
exit 0
```

A script may make life easier for the operator by providing a simplified selection for a more complex piece of code. Even though the script becomes gradually more complex to meet the requirements, to the operator the execution is greatly simplified. It is our job to enable users to run more complex operations easily from the command line when creating scripts. Often, this will necessitate the addition of more complexity to our scripts; however, we will be rewarded with the reliability of the scripted application.

Creating the backup2.sh using elif

We can revisit the script that we created to run the earlier backup. This script, `$HOME/bin/backup.sh`, prompts the user for the file type and the directory in which to store the backup. The tools used for the backup are `find` and `cp`.

With this new-found knowledge, we can now allow the script to run the backup using the command `tar` and the level of compression selected by the operator. There is no requirement to select the file type, as the complete home directory will be backed up, with the exclusion of the backup directory itself.

The operator can select the compression based on three letters: H, M, and L. The selection will affect the options passed to the `tar` command and the backup file created. The selection of high uses `bzip2` compression, medium uses `gzip` compression, and low creates an uncompressed `tar` archive. The logic exists in the extended `if` statement that follows:

```
if [ $file_compression = "L" ] ; then
tar_opt=$tar_l
elif [ $file_compression = "M" ]; then
tar_opt=$tar_m
else
tar_opt=$tar_h
fi
```

Based on the user selection, we can configure the correct options for the `tar` command. As we have three conditions to evaluate, the `if`, `elif`, and `else` statements are appropriate. To see how the variables are configured we can look at the following extract from the script:

```
tar_l="-cvf $backup_dir/b.tar --exclude $backup_dir $HOME"
tar_m="-czvf $backup_dir/b.tar.gz --exclude $backup_dir $HOME"
tar_h="-cjvf $backup_dir/b.tar.bzip2 --exclude $backup_dir $HOME"
```

The complete script can be created as `$HOME/bin/backup2.sh` and should comprise the following code:

```
#!/bin/bash
# Author: @theurbanpenguin
# Web: www.theurbapenguin.com
read -p "Choose H, M or L compression " file_compression
read -p "Which directory do you want to backup to " dir_name
# The next lines creates the directory if it does not exist
test -d $HOME/$dir_name || mkdir -m 700 $HOME/$dir_name
backup_dir=$HOME/$dir_name
tar_l="-cvf $backup_dir/b.tar --exclude $backup_dir $HOME"
tar_m="-czvf $backup_dir/b.tar.gz --exclude $backup_dir $HOME"
tar_h="-cjvf $backup_dir/b.tar.bzip2 --exclude $backup_dir $HOME"
if [ $file_compression = "L" ] ; then
tar_opt=$tar_l
elif [ $file_compression = "M" ]; then
tar_opt=$tar_m
else
tar_opt=$tar_h
```

```
fi
tar $tar_opt
exit 0
```

When we execute the script, we need to select H, M, or L in upper case, as this is how the selection is made within the script. The following screenshot shows the initial script execution, where the selection for M has been made:

```
pi@pilabs ~ $ backup2.sh
Choose H, M or L compression M_
```

Using case statements

Rather than using multiple elif statements, a case statement may provide a simpler mechanism when evaluations are made on a single expression.

The basic layout of a case statement is listed as follows, using pseudocode:

```
case expression in
  case1)
    statement1
    statement2
  ;;
  case2)
    statement1
    statement2
  ;;
  *)
    statement1
  ;;
esac
```

The statement layout that we see is not dissimilar to the switch statements that exist in other languages. In bash, we can use the case statement to test for simple values, such as strings or integers. Case statements can cater for a wide range of letters, such as [a-f] or a through to f, but they cannot easily deal with integer ranges such as [1-20].

The `case` statement will first expand the expression and then it will try to match it with each item in turn. When a match is found, all the statements are executed until the `;;`. This indicates the end of the code for that match. If there is no match, the case `else` statement indicated by the `*` will be matched. This needs to be the last item in the list.

Consider the following script `grade.sh`, which is used to evaluate grades:

```bash
#!/bin/bash
#Script to evaluate grades
#Usage: grade.sh stduent grade
#Author: @likegeeks
#Date: 1/1/1971
if [ ! $# -eq 2 ] ; then
    echo "You must provide <student> <grade>"
    exit 2
fi
case ${2^^} in #Parameter expansion is used to capitalize input
    [A-C]) echo "$1 is a star pupil"
    ;;
    [D]) echo "$1 needs to try a little harder!"
    ;;
    [E-F]) echo "$1 could do a lot better next year"
    ;;
    *) echo "Grade could not be evaluated for $1 $2"
    ;;
esac
```

The script first uses an `if` statement to check that exactly two arguments have been supplied to the script. If they are not supplied, the script will exit with an error state:

```bash
if [ ! $# -eq2 ] ; then
echo "You must provide <student><grade>
exit 2
fi
```

Then we use parameter expansion for the value of the `$2` variable to capitalize the input using `^^`. This represents the grade that we supply. Since we are capitalizing the input, we first try to match against the letters A through to C.

We make similar tests for the other supplied grades, E through to F.

The following screenshot shows the script execution with different grades:

```
pi@pilabs ~/bin $ grade.sh Bob b
Bob is a star pupil
pi@pilabs ~/bin $ grade.sh Bob D
Bob needs to try a little harder!
pi@pilabs ~/bin $ grade.sh Bob e
Bob could do a lot better next year
pi@pilabs ~/bin $ grade.sh Bob 5
Grade could not be evaluated for Bob 5
pi@pilabs ~/bin $ _
```

Recipe – building a frontend with grep

As a finale to this chapter, we will group a few features that we have learned together and build a script that prompts the operator for a filename, a search string, and an operation to carry out with the grep command. We will create the script as $HOME/bin/search.sh, and don't forget to make it executable:

```
#!/bin/bash
#Author: @theurbanpenguin
usage="Usage: search.sh file string operation"

if [ ! $# -eq3 ] ; then
echo "$usage"
exit 2
fi

[ ! -f $1 ] && exit 3

case $3 in
    [cC])
mesg="Counting the matches in $1 of $2"
opt="-c"
    ;;
    [pP])
mesg="Print the matches of $2 in $1"
        opt=""
    ;;
    [dD])
mesg="Printing all lines but those matching $3 from $1"
opt="-v"
    ;;
    *) echo "Could not evaluate $1 $2 $3";;
```

```
esac
echo $mesg
grep $opt $2 $1
```

We start by checking for exactly three input arguments using the following code:

```
if [ ! $# -eq3 ] ; then
echo "$usage"
exit 2
fi
```

The next check uses a command-line list to exit the script if the file argument is not a regular file, using `test -f`:

```
[ ! -f $1 ]&& exit 3
```

The `case` statement allows for three operations:

- Counting the matching lines
- Printing the matching lines
- Printing all but the matching lines

The following screenshot shows the search of the `/etc/ntp.conf` file for lines beginning with the string server. We choose the count option in this example:

```
pi@pilabs ~ $ search.sh /etc/ntp.conf ^server c
Counting the matches in /etc/ntp.conf of ^server
4
pi@pilabs ~ $ _
```

Summary

One of the most important and time-consuming tasks in scripting is building all of the conditional statements that we need to make the script usable and robust. There is an 80/20 rule that is often spoken of. This is where 20 percent of your time is spent in writing the main script and 80 percent of the time is spent in ensuring that all of the possible eventualities are correctly handled in the script. This is what we refer to as the procedural integrity of the script, where we try to cover each scenario carefully and accurately.

We started by looking at a simple test with command-line lists. If the actions needed are simple, then these provide great functionality and are easily added. Where more complexity is required, we add `if` statements.

Using the `if` statements, we can extend them as required using the `else` and `elif` keywords. Don't forget that `elif` keywords need their own conditions to evaluate.

We saw how to use `if` statements with the `test` command, and check strings, files, and numbers.

Finally, we saw how we can use `case` where a single expression needs to be evaluated.

In the next chapter, we will seek to understand the importance of reading in already prepared code snippets. We will create a sample `if` statement that can be saved as a code snippet to be read into the script at the time of editing.

Questions

1. What is the result of the following code: `True` or `False`?

```
if [ "LikeGeeks" \> "likegeeks" ]
then
echo "True"
else
echo "False"
fi
```

2. Which one of the following scripts is correct?

```
#!/bin/bash
if ! [ "mokhtar" = "Mokhtar" ]
then
echo "Strings are not identical"
else
echo "Strings are identical"
fi
```

Or

```
#!/bin/bash
if [ "mokhtar" != "Mokhtar" ]
then
echo "Strings are not identical"
else
echo "Strings are identical"
fi
```

3. How many commands can be used as an operator to return `True` in the following example?

```
#!/bin/bash
if [ 20 ?? 15 ]
then
echo "True"
else
echo "False"
fi
```

4. What is the result of the following code?

```
#!/bin/bash
mydir=/home/mydir
name="mokhtar"
if [ -d $mydir ] || [ -n $name ]; then
    echo "True"
else
echo "False"
fi
```

Further reading

Please see the following for further reading relating to this chapter:

- http://tldp.org/HOWTO/Bash-Prog-Intro-HOWTO-6.html
- http://tldp.org/LDP/Bash-Beginners-Guide/html/sect_07_03.html
- http://wiki.bash-hackers.org/commands/classictest

Creating Code Snippets

4

Now we can write our conditional tests to make decisions. After your hands become faster in coding, you will need to save some code pieces for later use, so how to save time and effort when writing scripts?

If you like using the command line, but also like some of the features associated with using graphical **integrated development environments (IDEs)**, then this chapter may reveal some new ideas to you. We can create shortcuts for commonly used script elements using the vi or vim text editors from the command line.

In this chapter, we will cover the following topics:

- Abbreviations
- Using code snippets
- Creating snippets using VS Code

Technical requirements

The source code for this chapter can be downloaded from here:

```
https://github.com/PacktPublishing/Mastering-Linux-Shell-Scripting-Second-
Edition/tree/master/Chapter04
```

Abbreviations

We have already taken one short sojourn into the ~/.vimrc file and we will now revisit this file to look at abbreviations or abbr controls. This file acts as the run control mechanism for the vim text editor, which is likely to be installed on your Linux distribution. Older distributions or Unix variants may have the original vi text editor and will make use of the ~/.exrc file. If you are uncertain of the identity of your version of vi and the correct run control file to use, simply enter the vi command. If a blank page opens, it is indeed vi. However, if a new blank document opens with the vim splash screens, then you are using the improved vim or vi.

Abbreviations allow for a shortcut string to be used in place of a longer string. These abbreviations can be set during a vim session from the last line mode but are often set in the control file. The shebang can be easily represented by an abbreviation, as follows:

```
abbr _sh #!/bin/bash
```

The basic syntax of an abbreviation is shown in the following command:

```
abbr <shortcut><string>
```

Using this abbreviation, we just need to type _sh while in the edit mode. On pressing the *Enter* key after the shortcut code, the full text for the shebang is printed. In reality, pressing any key after the abbr code will expand the shortcut, not just pressing the *Enter* key. Simple elements like this can add a lot to the experience of using vim as our text editor. The following screenshot shows the updated ~/.vimrc file:

```
pi@pilabs: ~
set showmode nohlsearch
set autoindent tabstop=4
set expandtab
syntax on
abbr _sh #!/bin/bash
```

We are not limited to the single abbreviation code, as we can add more abbr entries, for example, to support the shebang for Perl scripts at the line:

```
abbr _pl #!/usr/bin/perl
```

The use of the underscore is not required, but the aim is to keep the shortcut code unique and not to have a typed error. We are also not limited to a single line, although this is where abbreviations are most used. Consider the following abbreviation for an `if` statement:

```
abbr _if if [-z $1];then<CR>echo "> $0 <name><CR>exit 2<CR>fi
```

Although this does work, the formatting of the `if` statement will not be perfect and multiline abbreviations are far from ideal. This is where we may consider using code snippets that we have prepared in advance.

Using code snippets

All we mean by the term *code snippets* is a prepared code that we can read into our current script. This is especially easy with vim being able to read the contents of other text files during editing:

```
ESC
:r <path-and-filename>
```

For example, if we need to read the contents of a file called `if` located in `$HOME/snippets`, we will use the following key sequences in vim:

```
ESC
:r $HOME/snippets/if
```

The contents of this file are read into the current document below the current cursor position. In this way, we can make the code snippets as complex as we need and maintain the correct indentations to aide readability and consistency.

So, we will make it our duty to always create a snippets directory in our `home` directory:

```
$ mkdir -m 700 $HOME/snippets
```

It is not required to share the directory, so it is good practice to set the mode to `700` or private to the user when it is being created.

When creating snippets, it is your choice to use a pseudo-code or real examples. My preference is to use real examples that are edited to reflect the requirements of the recipient script. The contents of a simple `if` snippet will be as follows:

```
if [ -z $1 ] ; then
    echo "Usage: $0 <name>"
    exit 2
fi
```

This gives us the layout to create an `if` statement with a practical example. In this case, we check to see whether `$1` is unset and send an error to the user before exiting the script. The key is in keeping the snippet short to limit the changes that need to be made but make it easily understood and expandable as required.

Bringing color to the Terminal

If we are to display text messages to the users and operators executing the scripts, we can provide colors to help in message interpretation. Using red as a synonym for errors and green to indicate success makes it easier to add functionality to our scripts. Not all but certainly a vast majority of Linux Terminals support color. The built-in command `echo`, when used with the `-e` option, can display color to users.

To display a text in red, we can use the `echo` command as follows:

```
$ echo -e "\033[31mError\033[0m"
```

The following screenshot shows both the code and the output:

```
pi@pilabs ~ $ echo -e "\033[31mError\033[0m"
Error
```

The red text will bring immediate attention to the text and the potential failure of the script execution. The use of color in this way adheres to the basic principles of application design. If you find the code cumbersome, then simply use friendly variables to represent the colors and the reset code.

In the previous code, we used red and the final reset code to set the text back to the shell default. We could easily create variables for these color codes and others:

```
RED="\033[31m"
GREEN="\033[32m"
BLUE="\033[34m"
RESET="\033[0m"
```

 The `\033` value is the escape character and `[31m` is the color code for red.

We need to take care while using variables, to ensure that they are properly delimited from the text. Modifying the earlier example, we can see how this is easily achieved:

```
$ echo -e ${RED}Error$RESET"
```

We use the brace brackets to ensure that the RED variable is identified and separated from the Error word.

Saving the variable definitions to the $HOME/snippets/color file will allow them to be used in other scripts. Interestingly, we don't need to edit this script; we can use the command source to read these variables definitions into the script at runtime. Within the recipient script, we need to add the following line:

```
source $HOME/snippets/color
```

Using the shell built-in source command will read the color variables into the script that is executing at runtime. The following screenshot shows a modified version of the hello5.sh script that we now call hello7.sh, which makes use of these colors:

```
#!/bin/bash
# Welcome script to display a message to users on login
# Author: @theurbanpenguin
# Date: 1/1/1971
source $HOME/snippets/color
if [ $# -lt 1 ] ; then
   echo -e "${RED}Usage: $0 <name>$RESET"
   exit 1
fi
echo -e "${GREEN}Hello $1$RESET"
exit 0
```

We can see the effect this has when we execute the script. In the following screenshot, you will see the execution and output both with and without a supplied parameter:

```
pi@pilabs ~/bin $ hello7.sh fred
Hello fred
pi@pilabs ~/bin $ hello7.sh
Usage: /home/pi/bin/hello7.sh <name>
pi@pilabs ~/bin $ _
```

We can easily identify the success and failure of the script through the color-coded output; the green `Hello fred` where we supply the parameter, and the red `Usage` statement where we have not provided the required name.

Creating snippets using VS Code

For those who love graphical IDEs, you can use VS Code as an editor for your shell scripts. We used it as a debugger in `Chapter 1`, *The What and Why of Scripting with Bash*. Now we will see one of its capabilities as an editor.

You can create your own snippets in VS Code as follows.

Navigate to **File | Preferences | User Snippets**.

Then start to type `shell`. This will open the `shellscript.json` file.

The file has two brackets ready to enter your snippets between them:

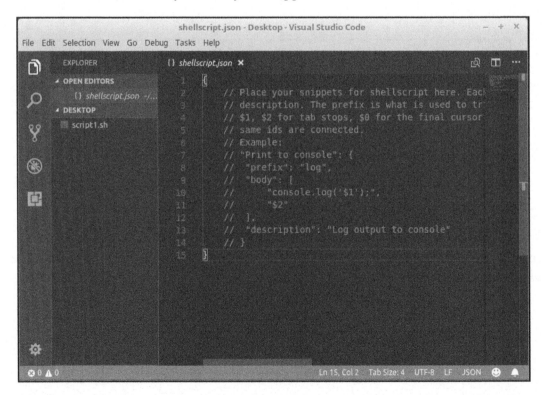

To create a snippet, type the following between the brackets on the file:

```
"Print a welcome message": {
    "prefix": "welcome",
    "body": [
        "echo 'Welcome to shell scripting!' "
    ],
    "description": "Print welcome message"
}
```

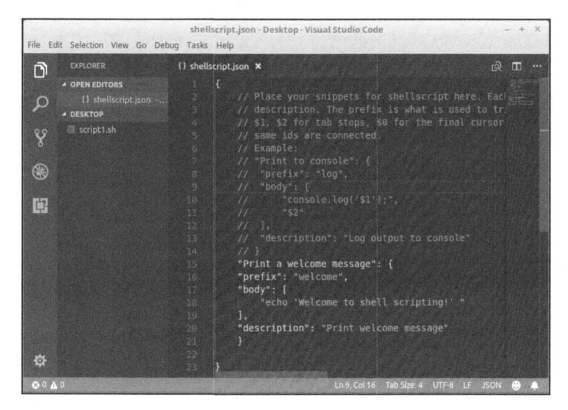

You can use the following template and modify it based on your needs.

Try to use prefixes different to the shell scripting keywords to avoid confusion.

When you open any `.sh` file and start to type `welcome`, the autocompletion will show you the snippet we have just created:

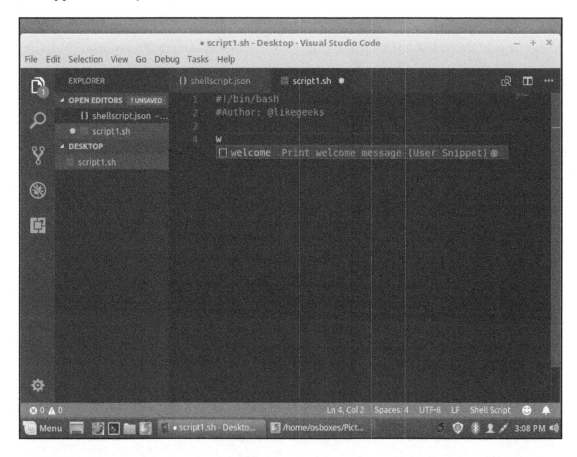

You can use any prefix you want; in our case, we used `welcome` so the autocompletion starts with it.

You can add many lines to your snippet body:

```
"Print to a welcome message": {
    "prefix": "welcome",
    "body": [
      "echo 'Welcome to shell scripting!' ",
      "echo 'This is a second message'"
    ],
    "description": "Print welcome message"
  }
```

You can use placeholders in your snippet body to simplify code editing.

Placeholders are written like this:

```
$1, $2, etc,
```

Modify the previous snippet and add a placeholder like this:

```
"Print a welcome message": {
  "prefix": "welcome",
  "body": [
    "echo 'Welcome to shell scripting! $1' "
  ],
  "description": "Print welcome message"
  }
```

When you start to type `welcome` and after you choose the snippet, you will notice that the cursor will stop at the exact position of the placeholder waiting for your input.

You can use choices if you forget what to type in these editable places:

```
"Print to a welcome message": {
  "prefix": "welcome",
  "body": [
    "echo 'Welcome to shell scripting! ${1|first,second,third|}' "
  ],
  "description": "Print welcome message"
  }
```

After you choose this snippet in your code and hit *Enter*, you should see the cursor waiting for your input with your choices:

That's very helpful!

Also, you can add a default value for the placeholder so this value will be written if you hit *Tab*:

```
"Print a welcome message": {
  "prefix": "welcome",
  "body": [
    "echo 'Welcome to shell scripting! ${1:book}' "
  ],
  "description": "Print welcome message"
  }
```

Summary

To any administrator, script reuse will always be upmost in the quest for efficiency. Using vim at the command line can make for very quick and effective editing of a script and we can save typing in the use of abbreviations. These are best set within a user's personal .vimrc file and are defined with the abbr control. Beyond abbreviations, we can see the sense in using code snippets. These are pre-prepared blocks of code that can be read into the current script.

Also, we had a look at the value in using color at the command line where a script will provide feedback. In the first look, these color codes are not the friendliest, but we can simplify the process by using variables. We created variables with color codes and saved them to a file and by using source command, these variables will be available to our current environment.

Finally, we saw how to create code snippets using VS Code and how to add placeholders to simplify our code editing.

In the next chapter, we will look at other mechanisms that we can use to write test expressions simplifying the use of integers and variables.

Questions

1. The following code creates a snippet which prints one line. How do you make the snippet with choices?

```
"Hello message": {
  "prefix": "hello",
  "body": [
    "echo 'Hello $1' "
  ],
  "description": "Hello message"
  }
```

2. Which command should you use to make your code snippets available for your use in the shell?

Further reading

Please see the following for further reading relating to this chapter:

- https://code.visualstudio.com/docs/editor/userdefinedsnippets
- https://brigade.engineering/sharpen-your-vim-with-snippets-767b693886db

Alternative Syntax

5

So far in the scripting journey, we have seen that we can use the `test` command to determine a conditional status. We have taken this a little further and discovered that we can also make use of the single square bracket. Here, we will recap the `test` command and look at the single square bracket in more detail. After having learned more about the square bracket, we will move onto more advanced variable or parameter management, thus providing defaults and understating quoting issues.

Finally, we are going to see that within advanced shells such as bash, Korn, and Zsh, we can go with double brackets! Making use of the double round parenthesis and double square bracket can simplify the overall syntax and allow the standardization of the use of mathematical symbols.

In this chapter, we will cover the following topics:

- Recapping `test`
- Providing parameter defaults
- When in doubt – quote!
- Advanced tests using `[[`
- Arithmetic operations using `((`

Technical requirement

The source code for this chapter can be downloaded from here:

```
https://github.com/PacktPublishing/Mastering-Linux-Shell-Scripting-Second-
Edition/tree/master/Chapter05
```

Recapping the test command

So far, we have used the built-in `test` command to drive our conditional statements. Using other options with `test`, we can look at the returned value to determine the status of files in the filesystem. Running the `test` command without any options will return a false output:

```
$ test
```

Testing files

Commonly, we can use `test` to check the conditions based around files. For example, to test whether a file is present or not, we can use the -e option. The following command will test the existence of the /etc/hosts file:

```
test -e /etc/hosts
```

We can run this `test` again, but this time check that the file not only exists but is a regular file as opposed to having some special purpose. Specific file types can be directories, pipes, and links, among others. The option for a regular file is -f:

```
$ test -f /etc/hosts
```

Adding logic

If we need to open a file from within our script, we test that the file is both a regular file and has the read permission set. To achieve this with `test`, we can also include the -a option to AND multiple conditions together. In the following example command, we will use the -r condition to check that the file is readable:

```
$ test -f /etc/hosts -a -r /etc/hosts
```

Similarly, the use of -o is supported to OR two conditions within an expression.

Square brackets as not seen before

As an alternative to the `test` command, we can implement the same conditional tests using the single square bracket. Repeating the previous conditional `test` and omitting the command itself. We will rewrite this, as shown in the following command:

```
$ [ -f /etc/hosts -a -r /etc/hosts ]
```

Many times, even as experienced administrators, we are used to language elements and we accept them as they are. I feel many Linux administrators will be surprised to learn that [is a command for both a shell built-in and a standalone file. Using the `type` command, we can verify this:

```
$ type -a [
```

We can see the output of this command in the following screenshot confirming its existence:

```
pi@pilabs ~ $ type -a [
[ is a shell builtin
[ is /usr/bin/[
pi@pilabs ~ $
```

The built-in [command imitates the `test` command but it requires a closing bracket.

Now we know a little more about the [command, which is found in bash and the earlier Bourne shell, we can now continue to add a little command-line list syntax. In addition to the command-line list, we can see the desired functionality working in the following command sample:

```
$ FILE=/etc/hosts
$ [ -f $FILE -a -r $FILE ] && cat $FILE
```

Having set the parameter `FILE` variable, we can test that it is both a regular file and is readable by the user before attempting to list the file contents. In this way, the script becomes more robust without the need for a complex script logic. We can see the code in use in the following screenshot:

```
pi@pilabs ~ $ FILE=/etc/hosts
pi@pilabs ~ $ [ -f $FILE -a -r $FILE ] && cat $FILE
127.0.0.1       localhost
::1             localhost ip6-localhost ip6-loopback
fe00::0         ip6-localnet
ff00::0         ip6-mcastprefix
ff02::1         ip6-allnodes
ff02::2         ip6-allrouters

#127.0.1.1      pilabs.theurbanpenguin.com
pi@pilabs ~ $
```

This type of abbreviation is quite common and is easily recognizable. We should always be cautious of using abbreviations if they do not add readability. Our aim in scripting should be to write clear and understandable code and avoid shortcuts if they do not add to this goal.

Providing parameter defaults

Within bash parameters, there are named spaces in the memory that allow us access to stored values. There are two types of parameters:

- Variables
- Special parameters

Variables

We already described what variables are and how to define them in Chapter 1, *The What and Why of Scripting with Bash*.

Just to refresh your memory, you can define a variable by assigning a value with an equals sign and without any spaces like this:

```
#!/bin/bash
myvar=15
myvar2="welcome"
```

So nothing new here.

Special parameters

Special parameters are the second parameter type and are managed by the shell itself and are presented as read-only. We have come across these before in parameters such as $0 but let's take a look at another $-. We can expand these parameters to gain an understanding of their use, using the echo command:

```
$ echo "My shell is $0 and the shell options are: $-"
```

From the annotated text that I have added, we can understand that the $-$ option represents the shell options that are configured. These can be displayed using the set -o command but it can be read programmatically using $-$.

We can see this in the following screenshot:

```
pi@pilabs ~ $ echo "I am using $0 with the options: $-"
I am using -bash with the options: himBH
pi@pilabs ~ $ _
```

The options set here are as follows:

- h: This is short for hashall; it allows for programs to be found using the PATH parameter
- i: This shows that this is an interactive shell
- m: This is short for monitor; it allows the use of the bg and fg commands to bring commands in and out of the background
- B: This allows the brace expansion or mkdirdir{1,2}, where we create dir1 and dir2
- H: This allows history expansion of running commands, such as !501 to repeat commands from history

Setting defaults

Using either the test command or the brackets, we can provide default values for variables, including command-line parameters. Taking the hello4.sh script we worked with earlier, we can modify it and set the name parameter if it is zero bytes:

```
#!/bin/bash
name=$1
[ -z $name ] && name="Anonymous"
echo "Hello $name"
exit 0
```

This code is functional but it is our choice how we code in the default value. We can, alternatively, assign a default value directly to the parameter. Consider the following command, where a default assignment is made directly:

```
name=${1-"Anonymous"}
```

In bash, this is known as **parameter substitution** and can be written in the following pseudo-code:

```
${parameter-default}
```

Wherever a variable (parameter) has not been declared and has a null value, the default value will be used. If the parameter has been explicitly declared with a null value, we will use the : – syntax, as shown in the following example:

```
parameter=
${parameter:-default}
```

By editing the script now, we can create hello8.sh to make use of bash parameter substitution to provide the default value:

```
#!/bin/bash
#Use parameter substitution to provide default value
name=${1-"Anonymous"}
echo "Hello $name"
exit 0
```

This script and its output, both with and without a supplied value, are shown in the following screenshot:

```
pi@pilabs ~ $ hello8.sh
Hello Anonymous
pi@pilabs ~ $ hello8.sh   fred
Hello fred
pi@pilabs ~ $ cat bin/hello8.sh
#!/bin/bash
name=${1-"Anonymous"}
echo "Hello $name"
exit 0
pi@pilabs ~ $ _
```

The hello8.sh script provides the functionality that we need, with the logic built directly into the parameter assignment. The logic and assignment are now a single line of code within the script and this is a major step in keeping the script simple and maintaining the readability.

When in doubt – quote!

Having established that variables are a type of parameter, we should always keep this in mind, especially when reading manuals and *HOWTOs*. Often the documentation refers to parameters and, in doing so, they include variables, as well as the bash special parameters, such as $1 and so on. In keeping with this, we will look at why it is advisable to quote the parameters when we use them on the command line or within scripts. Learning this now can save us a lot of pain and heartache later, especially when we start looking at loops.

First, the correct term that we should use for reading the value of variables is **parameter expansion**. To you and me, this is reading a variable, but to bash this would be too simple. The assignment of a correct name, such as parameter expansion, reduces any ambiguity to its meaning but adds complexity at the same time. In the following example, the first line of command assigns the value of fred to the name parameter. The second line of command uses parameter expansion to print the stored value from memory. The $ symbol is used to allow the expansion of the parameter:

```
$ name=fred
$ echo "The value is: $name"
```

In the example, we have used the double quotes to allow echo to print the single string as we have used spaces. Without the use of quotes, echo might have seen this as multiple arguments, the space being the default field separator in most shells, including bash. Often, when we do not think to use quotes, we do not see the spaces directly. Consider the following extract of command-line code that we made use of earlier:

```
$ FILE=/etc/hosts
$ [ -f $FILE -a -r $FILE ] && cat $FILE
```

Even though this worked, we may have been a little fortunate, especially if we were populating the FILE parameter from a list of files that we had not created ourselves. It is quite conceivable that a file can have spaces within its name. Let's now replay this command using a different file. Consider the following command:

```
$ FILE="my file"
$ [ -f $FILE -a -r $FILE ] && cat $FILE
```

Even though, structurally, there has been no change to the code, it now fails. This is because we are providing too many arguments to the [command. The failing result will be the same even if we use the test command.

Even though we have correctly quoted the assignment of the filename to the parameter
FILE, we have not protected the spaces when the parameter is expanded. We can see the
code failing, as it is captured in the following screenshot:

```
pi@pilabs ~ $ FILE="my file"
pi@pilabs ~ $ [ -f $FILE -a -r $FILE ] && cat $FILE
-bash: [: too many arguments
pi@pilabs ~ $
```

We can see that this will not be ready for our scripts. Alas, what we once thought of as
robust is now in tatters and, like the Titanic, our code has sunk.

However, a simple solution is to revert to quoting parameter expansion unless specifically
not desired. We can make this ship unsinkable with a simple edit to the code:

```
$ FILE="my file"
$ [ -f "$FILE" -a -r "$FILE" ] && cat "$FILE"
```

We can now proudly stand on the White Star Line dock, as we see the Titanic II get
launched in the following code example, which is captured in the following screenshot:

```
pi@pilabs ~ $ FILE="my file"
pi@pilabs ~ $ [ -f "$FILE" -a -r "$FILE" ] && cat "$FILE"
The File Contents
pi@pilabs ~ $
```

It is truly amazing and sometimes just a little unbelievable what effect these tiny quotes can
have. We should never ignore the quotes when expanding variables. To ensure that we drill
home this point, we can highlight this phenomenon in another, even simpler, example. Let's
take the scenario where we now just want to remove the file. In the first example, we do not
use quotes:

```
$ rm $FILE
```

This code will produce failures as the parameter expansion will lead to the following
perceived command:

```
$ rm my file
```

The code will fail because it is unable to find the `my` file or the `file` file. Even worse, we could potentially be deleting incorrect files if any of the names could be resolved accidentally. However, quoting the parameter expansion will save the day, as we see in the second example:

```
$ rm "$FILE"
```

This is correctly expanded to the desired command that we illustrate in the following command example:

```
$ rm "my file"
```

I certainly hope that these examples demonstrate the need for care when expanding parameters and make you aware of the pitfalls.

Advanced tests using [[

The use of the double brackets `[[ condition ]]` allows us to do more advanced condition testing but it is not compatible with the Bourne shell. The double brackets were first introduced as a defined keyword in the KornShell and are also available in bash and Zsh. Unlike the single bracket, this is not a command but a keyword. The use of the `type` command can confirm this:

```
$ type [[
```

White space

The fact that `[[` is not a command is significant where white space is concerned. As a keyword, `[[` parses its arguments before bash expands them. As such, a single parameter will always be represented as a single argument. Even though it goes against best practice, `[[` can alleviate some of the issues associated with white space within parameter values. Reconsidering the condition we tested earlier, we can omit the quotes when using `[[`, as shown in the following example:

```
$ echo "The File Contents">"my file"
$ FILE="my file"
$ [[ -f $FILE && -r $FILE ]] && cat "$FILE"
```

We still need to quote the parameter when using `cat`, as you can see, and we can use quotes within the double brackets but they become optional. Note that we can also use the more traditional `&&` and `||` to represent `-a` and `-o` respectively.

Other advanced features

These are some of the extra features that we can include with the double brackets. Even if we lose portability in using them, there are some great features that overcome the loss. Remember that if we only use bash, then we can use the double brackets but can't run our scripts in the Bourne shell. The advanced features that we gain, which are covered in the following sections, include pattern matching and regular expressions.

Pattern matching

Using the double brackets, we can do more than just match strings, we can use pattern matching. For example, we may need to work exclusively with Perl scripts, files that end with .pl. We will be able to implement this easily within a condition by including the pattern as a match, as shown in the following example:

```
$ [[ $FILE = *.pl ]] && cp"$FILE" scripts/
```

Regular expressions

We will talk in dept about regular expressions in a Chapter 11, *Regular Expressions*, but let's take a small glimpse now.

We could rewrite the last example using a regular expression:

```
$ [[ $FILE =~ \.pl$ ]] && cp "$FILE" scripts/
```

As the single dot or period has a special meaning in regular expressions, we need to escape it with \.

The following screenshot shows the regular expression matching working with a file called my.pl and another called my.apl. The match correctly shows for the file that ends in .pl:

```
pi@pilabs ~ $ FILE="my.pl"
pi@pilabs ~ $ [[ $FILE =~ \.pl$ ]] && echo "Perl found"
Perl found
pi@pilabs ~ $ FILE="my.apl"
pi@pilabs ~ $ [[ $FILE =~ \.pl$ ]] && echo "Perl found"
pi@pilabs ~ $ _
```

Regular expression script

Another simple demonstration of conditional testing using regular expressions will be to expose the US and UK spelling of *color*, being *color* and *colour* respectively. We may prompt the user if they want a color or mono output for the script but at the same time cater for both spellings. The line that will do the work in the script is as follows:

```
if [[ $REPLY =~ colou?r ]] ; then
```

The regular expression caters to both spellings of *color* by making the u optional: u?. Furthermore, we can disable case sensitivity allowing for *COLOR* and *color* by setting a shell option:

```
shopt -s nocasematch
```

This option can be disabled again at the end of the script with the following command:

```
shopt -u nocasematch
```

When we use the variable parameters that we have named $GREEN and $RESET, we affect the color of the output. The color green will only be shown where we have sourced the color definition file. This is set when we choose the color display. Selecting mono will ensure that the variable parameters are null and have no effect.

The complete script is shown in the following screenshot:

```
#!/bin/bash
# Welcome script to display a message to users on login
# Author: @theurbanpenguin
# Date: 1/1/1971
shopt -s nocasematch #turn off case sensitivity
read -p "Type color or mono for script output: "
if [[ $REPLY =~ colou?r ]] ; then
  source $HOME/snippets/color
fi
#Where parameters are not set the display will be mono
echo -e "${GREEN}This is $0 $RESET"
shopt -u nocasematch #reset case sensitivity
exit 0
```

Arithmetic operations using ((

When using bash and some other advanced shells, we can make use of the (( )) notation to simplify mathematical operations with scripts.

Simple math

The double parenthesis construct in bash allows for arithmetic expansion. Using this in the simplest format, we can easily carry out integer arithmetic. This becomes a replacement for the let built-in. The following examples show the use of the let command and the double parenthesis to achieve the same result:

```
$ a=(( 2 + 3 ))
$ let a=2+3
```

In both cases, the a parameter is populated with the sum of 2 + 3. If you want to write it on a shell script, you need to add a dollar sign before the parentheses:

```
#!/bin/bash
echo $(( 2 + 3 ))
```

Parameter manipulation

Perhaps a little more useful to us in scripting is the C-style parameter manipulation that we can include using the double parenthesis. We can often use this to increment a counter within a loop and also put a limit on the number of times the loop iterates. Consider the following command:

```
$ COUNT=1
$ (( COUNT++ ))
echo $COUNT
```

Within this example, we first set COUNT to 1 and then we increment it with the ++ operator. When it is echoed in the final line, the parameter will have a value of 2. We can see the results in the following screenshot:

```
pi@pilabs ~/bin $ COUNT=1
pi@pilabs ~/bin $ (( COUNT++ ))
pi@pilabs ~/bin $ echo $COUNT
2
pi@pilabs ~/bin $ _
```

We can achieve the same result in longhand by using the following syntax:

```
$ COUNT=1
$ (( COUNT=COUNT+1 ))
echo $COUNT
```

This of course allows for any increment of the COUNT parameter and not just a single unit increase. Similarly, we can count down using the -- operator, as shown in the following example:

```
$ COUNT=10
$ (( COUNT-- ))
echo $COUNT
```

We start using a value of 10, reducing the value by 1 within the double parentheses.

 Note that we do not use the $ to expand the parameters within the parentheses. They are used for parameter manipulation and, as such, we do not need to expand parameters explicitly.

Standard arithmetic tests

Another advantage that we can gain from these double parentheses is with the tests. Rather than having to use -gt for greater than, we can simply use >. We can demonstrate this in the following code:

```
$(( COUNT > 1 )) && echo "Count is greater than 1"
```

The following screenshot demonstrates this:

```
pi@pilabs ~/bin $ COUNT=10
pi@pilabs ~/bin $ (( COUNT-- ))
pi@pilabs ~/bin $ (( COUNT > 1 )) && echo "Count is greater than 1"
Count is greater than 1
pi@pilabs ~/bin $
```

It is this standardization, both in the C-style manipulation and tests, that makes the double parenthesis so useful to us. This use extends to both the command line and scripts. We will use this feature extensively when we look at looping constructs.

Summary

Within this chapter, I really hope that we have introduced many new and interesting choices to you. This was an area with a wide range where we began by recapping the use of test and discovered that the [is a command not a syntax construct. The main effect that it is a command is on white space and we looked at the need to quote variables.

Even though we may commonly call variables variables, we have also seen that their correct name, especially in documentation, is parameters. Reading a variable is a parameter expansion. Understanding parameter expansion can help us understand the use of the keyword [[. The double square brackets are not commands and do not expand the parameters. This means that we do not need to quote variables even if they do contain white space. Moreover, we can use advanced tests with double square brackets, such as pattern matching or regular expressions.

Finally, we looked at arithmetic expansion and parameter manipulation using the double parenthesis notation. The biggest feature this delivers is the possibility to easily increment and decrement counters.

In the next chapter, we will move onto the looping constructs found in bash and make use of some of our new-found skills from this chapter.

Questions

1. How do you subtract 8 from 25 using shell scripting?
2. What is wrong with the following code? And how can you fix it?

    ```
    $ rm my file
    ```

3. What is the problem with the following code?

    ```
    #!/bin/bash
    a=(( 8 + 4 ))
    echo $a
    ```

Further reading

Please see the following for further reading relating to this chapter:

- `http://tldp.org/LDP/abs/html/arithexp.html`
- `http://wiki.bash-hackers.org/commands/classictest`

Iterating with Loops

6

Now we can perform arithmetic operations and tests and our scripts have more control. Sometimes, you will find that you need to perform some tasks repeatedly, such as going through log file entries and performing an action, or maybe running a piece of code continuously. We are busy people who have better things to do than repeat a task 100 times or more; loops are our friends.

Looping structures are the lifeblood of scripts. These loops are workhorse engines that can iterate many times, repeating the same task reliably and consistently. Imagine having 100,000 lines of text within a CSV file that has to be checked for incorrect entries. A script can do this easily and accurately once developed but, in the case of a human, the reliability factor and accuracy will fail very quickly.

So let's see how we can save our time and sanity by covering the following topics in this chapter:

- `for` loops
- Advanced `for` loops
- The internal field separator (IFS)
- Counting directories and files
- C-style for loops
- Nested loops
- Redirecting loop output
- `while` loops and `until` loops
- Reading input from files
- Creating operator menus

Technical requirement

The source code for this chapter can be can be downloaded from here:

```
https://github.com/PacktPublishing/Mastering-Linux-Shell-Scripting-Second-
Edition/tree/master/Chapter06
```

for loops

All our looping controls are simple and we will begin by looking at for loops. The word for is a keyword in bash and in terms of its working, it is similar to if. We can use the command type to verify this, as shown in the following example:

```
$ type for
for is a shell keyword
```

As a reserved shell keyword, we can use a for loop both in scripts and directly at the command line. In this way, we can utilize loops within and without the scripts, optimizing the use of the command line. A simple for loop is shown in the following example code:

```
# for u in bob joe ; do
useradd $u
echo '$u:Password1' | chpasswd  #pipe the created user to chpasswd
passwd -e $u
done
```

The useradd command is used to create users and the chpasswd command is used to update passwords in batch mode.

Within a for loop, we read from the list on the right to populate the variable parameter on the left; in this case, we will read from the list containing bob and joe into the parameter variable u. Each item from the list is inserted into the variable, one item at a time. In this way, as long as there are items to be processed in the list, the loop will execute until the list is exhausted.

Practically, for us, the execution of this loop means that we will do the following:

1. Create the user bob
2. Set the password for bob
3. Expire the password so it will need to be reset on the first login for the user bob

We then loop back and repeat the process for the user joe.

We can view the preceding example in the following screenshot. After having gained root access through `sudo -i`, we proceeded to run the loop and create the users:

```
pi@pilabs ~ $ sudo -i
[sudo] password for pi:
root@pilabs:~# for u in bob joe ; do
> useradd $u
> echo "$u:Password1" | chpasswd
> passwd -e $u
> done
passwd: password expiry information changed.
passwd: password expiry information changed.
root@pilabs:~#
```

The list that is read in the `for` loop can be generated dynamically or statically, as shown in the previous example. To create dynamic lists, we could use various globbing techniques to populate the list. As an example, to work with all files in a directory, we could use `*`, as shown in the following example:

```
for f in * ; do
stat "$f"
done
```

> When a list is generated, such as with file globbing, we should quote the expansion of the variable parameter. Without the quotes, it is possible that a space will be included that will cause the command to fail. This is what we have seen here in the `stat` command.

In the following examples, we isolate the filenames that begin with `ba*`. We then use the `stat` command to print the inode metadata. The code and output are shown in the following screenshot:

```
pi@pilabs ~/bin $ for f in ba* ; do
> stat "$f"
> done
  File: `backup2.sh'
  Size: 675            Blocks: 8          IO Block: 4096    regular file
Device: b302h/45826d    Inode: 270110    Links: 1
Access: (0755/-rwxr-xr-x)  Uid: ( 1000/      pi)   Gid: ( 1000/      pi)
Access: 2015-07-17 14:00:04.119477594 +0000
Modify: 2015-07-17 14:00:04.119477594 +0000
Change: 2015-07-17 14:00:04.139477463 +0000
 Birth: -
  File: `backup.sh'
  Size: 775            Blocks: 8          IO Block: 4096    regular file
Device: b302h/45826d    Inode: 268466    Links: 1
Access: (0755/-rwxr-xr-x)  Uid: ( 1000/      pi)   Gid: ( 1000/      pi)
Access: 2015-07-04 19:56:11.481438080 +0000
Modify: 2015-07-04 19:56:11.481438080 +0000
Change: 2015-07-04 19:56:11.491438018 +0000
 Birth: -
```

This list can also be generated from the output of another command or a pipeline of commands. For example, if we need to print the current working directory of all logged-in users, we could try something similar to the following:

```
$ for user in $(who | cut -f1 -d" ") ; do
lsof -u "$user" -a -c bash | grep cwd
done
```

In the previous example, we can see that the choice of name for the parameter is down to us; we are not limited to a single character and we can use the $user name in this example. By using lowercase, we will not overwrite the system variable $USER. The following screenshot demonstrates the loop and the subsequent output:

```
pi@pilabs ~/bin $ for user in $(who | cut -f1 -d" ") ; do
> lsof -u "$user" -a -c bash | grep cwd
> done
bash    14935   pi  cwd   DIR  179,2    4096 268409 /home/pi/bin
bash    15140   pi  cwd   DIR  179,2    4096 268409 /home/pi/bin
pi@pilabs ~/bin $ ▮
```

The lsof command will list open files; we can search for the files opened by each user in turn and with the bash command as the current working directory.

Working with the scripts that we have created so far, we can create a new script called hello9.sh. If we copy the $HOME/bin/hello2.sh script to the new script, we can edit it to make use of a for loop:

```
#!/bin/bash
echo "You are using $(basename $0)"
for n in $*
do
        echo "Hello $n"
done
exit 0
```

The loop is used to iterate through each command-line argument supplied and greet each user individually. When we execute the script, we can see that we can now display the Hello message for each user. This is shown in the following screenshot:

```
pi@pilabs ~/bin $
pi@pilabs ~/bin $ hello9.sh fred bob
You are using hello9.sh
Hello fred
Hello bob
pi@pilabs ~/bin $
```

Although what we have seen here is still relatively trivial, we should now realize a little of what we can do with scripts and loops. The arguments of this script can be the usernames that we have already used or anything else. If we stick with the usernames, then it will be very easy to create user accounts and set passwords, as we saw earlier.

Advanced for loops

In the previous examples, we used the `for` loop to iterate over simple values where each value has no space.

As you know, if your values contain a space, you should use double quotes:

```
#!/bin/bash
for var in one "This is two" "Now three" "We'll check four"
do
echo "Value: $var"
done
```

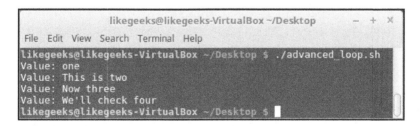

As you can see, each value is printed as expected thanks to double quotes.

This example contains values in one line and we quote the values because they have spaces and commas. What if the values were on multiple lines, as in a file?

What if the separator between the values we want to iterate over is something other than a space such as a comma or a semicolon?

Here comes the IFS.

The IFS

By default, the IFS variable has the value of one of (space, newline, or tab).

Suppose that you have a file like the following and you want to iterate over its lines:

```
Hello, this is a test
This is the second line
And this is the last line
```

Let's write the `for` loop that will iterate over these lines:

```
#!/bin/bash
file="file1.txt"
for var in $(cat $file)
do
echo " $var"
done
```

If you check the result, it's something that we don't need:

Since the first separator the shell found is the space, the shell treats every word as a field, but we need every line to be printed as a field.

Here we need to change the IFS variable to be newline instead.

Let's modify our script to iterate over lines correctly:

```
#!/bin/bash
file="file1.txt"
IFS=$'\n'    #Here we change the default IFS to be a newline
for var in $(cat $file)
do
echo " $var"
done
```

We changed the IFS variable to newline and it works as expected.

Look at the dollar sign in the IFS definition in the preceding section, `IFS=$"\n"`. By default, bash doesn't interpret escape characters such as `\r`, `\n`, and `\t`. So, in our example, it will be treated as an n character, so to interpret escape characters, you have to use a dollar sign ($) before it to make it work properly.

But if your IFS is a normal character, you don't have to use the dollar sign ($) at all.

Counting directories and files

We can use a simple `for` loop to iterate over folder content and use an `if` statement to check whether the path is a directory or a file:

```
#!/bin/bash
for path in /home/likegeeks/*
do
    if [ -d "$path" ]
    then
            echo "$path is a directory"
```

```
    elif [ -f "$path" ]
    then
          echo "$path is a file"
    fi
done
```

```
                likegeeks@likegeeks-VirtualBox ~/Desktop        —  +  ×

 File  Edit  View  Search  Terminal  Help
likegeeks@likegeeks-VirtualBox ~/Desktop $ ./count_files.sh
/home/likegeeks/book.pdf is a file
/home/likegeeks/Desktop is a directory
/home/likegeeks/Documents is a directory
/home/likegeeks/Downloads is a directory
/home/likegeeks/eclipse is a directory
/home/likegeeks/likegeeks is a directory
```

This is pretty straightforward script. We iterate over directory content and then we use an `if` statement to check whether the path is a directory or a file. Finally, we print beside each path whether it's a file or a directory.

> We used quotes for the path variable because the file could contain a space.

C-style for loops

If you have a C language background, you will be happy to know that you can write your `for` loops in C-style. This feature was taken from KornShell. The shell `for` loop can be written like this:

```
for (v= 0; v < 5; v++)
{
 printf(Value is %d\n", v);
}
```

It is easy for C developers to use this syntax in `for` loops.

Check out this example:

```
#!/bin/bash
for (( v=1; v <= 10; v++ ))
do
    echo "value is $v"
done
```

The choice is yours; you have a lot of syntax styles for the `for` loop.

Nested loops

Nested loops means loops inside loops. Check out the following example:

```
#!/bin/bash
for (( v1 = 1; v1 <= 3; v1++ ))
do
    echo "First loop $v1:"
    for (( v2 = 1; v2 <= 3; v2++ ))
    do
            echo " Second loop: $v2"
    done
done
```

The first loop hits first, then the second loop, and this happens three times.

Redirecting loop output

You can redirect the loop output to a file using the `done` command:

```
#!/bin/bash
for (( v1 = 1; v1 <= 5; v1++ ))
do
    echo "$v1"
done > file
```

If there is no file, it will be created and filled with the loop output.

This redirection is helpful when you don't need to show the loop output on the screen and save it to a file instead.

Controlling the loop

Having entered our loop, we may need to either exit the loop prematurely or perhaps exclude certain items from processing. If we want to process only directories in a listing, rather than every file of any type, then to implement this, we have loop control keywords, such as `break` and `continue`.

The `break` keyword is used to exit the loop, processing no more entries, whereas the `continue` keyword is used to stop the processing of the current entry in the loop and resume the processing with the next entry.

Assuming we only want to process directories, we could implement a test within the loop and determine the file type:

```
$ for f in * ; do
[ -d "$f" ] || continue
chmod 3777 "$f"
done
```

Within the loop, we want to set permissions, including the SGID and sticky bits, but for the directories only. The * search will return all files; the first statement within the loop will ensure that we only process directories. If the test is done for the current loop, the target fails the test and is not a directory; the `continue` keyword retrieves the next loop-list item. If the `test` returns `true` and we are working with a directory, then we will process the subsequent statements and execute the `chmod` command.

If we need to run the loop until we find a directory and then exit the loop, we can adjust the code so that we can iterate though each file. If the file is a directory, then we exit the loop with the break keyword:

```
$ for f in * ; do
[ -d "$f" ] && break
done
echo "We have found a directory $f"
```

Within the following screenshot, we can see the code in action:

```
pi@pilabs ~ $ for f in * ; do
> [ -d "$f" ] && break
> done
pi@pilabs ~ $ echo "We have found a directory: $f"
We have found a directory: bin
pi@pilabs ~ $
```

By working with the same theme, we can print each directory found in the listing using the following code:

```
for f in * ; do
[ -d "$f" ] || continue
dir_name="$dir_name $f"
done
echo "$dir_name"
```

We can achieve a result by processing the loop item only if it is a directory and within the loop. We can work with regular files only using the if test. In this example, we append the directory name to the dir_name variable. Once we exit the loop, we print the complete list of directories. We can see this in the following screenshot:

```
pi@pilabs ~ $ for f in * ; do [ -d "$f" ] || continue
> dir_list="$dir_list $f"
> done
pi@pilabs ~ $ echo "$dir_list"
 bin python_games snippets
pi@pilabs ~ $ _
```

Using these examples and your own ideas, you should now be able to see how you can control loops using the continue and break keywords.

while loops and until loops

When using the `for` loop, we iterate through a list; it's either the one that we create or the one that is dynamically generated. Using the `while` or `until` loops, we loop based on the fact that the condition becomes either `true` or `false`.

A `while` loop loops while the condition is true and, conversely, an `until` loop will loop while the condition is false. The following command will count from 10 through to zero, each iteration of the loop printing the variable and then reducing the value by one:

```
$ COUNT=10
$ while (( COUNT >= 0 )) ; do
echo -e "$COUNT \c"
(( COUNT-- ))
done ; echo
```

We can see the output of this command in the following screenshot, thus confirming the countdown to zero:

```
pi@pilabs ~ $ COUNT=10
pi@pilabs ~ $ while (( COUNT >= 0 )) ; do
> echo -e "$COUNT \c"
> (( COUNT-- ))
> done ; echo
10 9 8 7 6 5 4 3 2 1 0
pi@pilabs ~ $ _
```

 The use of the `\c` escape sequence used here allows the suppression of the line feed normally used with `echo`. In this way, we can keep the countdown on the single line of output. I think you will agree that it's a nice effect.

The functionality of this loop can be gained using the `until` loop; just a quick rethink of the logic is required, as we will want to loop until the condition becomes true. Generally, it is a personal choice and the way the logic works best for you about which loop to use. The following example shows the loop written with the `until` loop:

```
$ COUNT=10
$ until (( COUNT < 0 )) ; do
echo -e "$COUNT \c"
(( COUNT-- ))
done ; echo
```

Reading input from files

Now, it may seem that these loops can do a little more than just count down numbers. We may want to read data in from a text file and process each line. The shell built-in `read` command that we saw earlier in this book can be used to read a file line by line. In this way, we can use a loop to process each line of a file.

To demonstrate some of these functionalities, we will use a file that contains the server addresses. These could be hostnames or IP addresses. In the following example, we will make use of the IP addresses of Google DNS servers. The following command shows the contents of the `servers.txt` file:

```
$ cat servers.txt
8.8.8.8
8.8.4.4
```

Using the `read` command in the condition of the `while` loop, we can loop as long as we have more lines to read from the file. We specify the input file directly after the `done` keyword. For each line that we read from the file, we can test whether the server is up with the `ping` command, and, if the server is responding, we append it to a list of available servers. This list is printed once the loop closes. In the following example, we can see that we begin to add in as many elements of scripting as we have covered in this book:

```
$ while read server ; do
ping -c1 $server && servers_up="$servers_up $server"
done < servers.txt
echo "The following servers are up: $servers_up"
```

We can verify the operation in the following screenshot, which captures the output:

```
pi@pilabs ~ $
pi@pilabs ~ $ cat servers.txt
8.8.8.8
8.8.4.4
pi@pilabs ~ $ while read server ; do
> ping -c1 "$server" && servers_up="$servers_up $servers"
> done < servers.txt
PING 8.8.8.8 (8.8.8.8) 56(84) bytes of data.
64 bytes from 8.8.8.8: icmp_req=1 ttl=52 time=25.1 ms

--- 8.8.8.8 ping statistics ---
1 packets transmitted, 1 received, 0% packet loss, time 0ms
rtt min/avg/max/mdev = 25.187/25.187/25.187/0.000 ms
PING 8.8.4.4 (8.8.4.4) 56(84) bytes of data.
64 bytes from 8.8.4.4: icmp_req=1 ttl=52 time=24.9 ms

--- 8.8.4.4 ping statistics ---
1 packets transmitted, 1 received, 0% packet loss, time 0ms
rtt min/avg/max/mdev = 24.950/24.950/24.950/0.000 ms
pi@pilabs ~ $ echo "These servers are up $servers_up"
These servers are up  8.8.8.8 8.8.4.4
pi@pilabs ~ $ _
```

Using this kind of loop, we can start to build extremely practical scripts to process information either fed from the command line or from scripts. It will be very easy to replace the filename that we read with $1, representing a positional parameter passed into the script. Let's return to the ping_server.sh script and adjust it to accept the input parameter. We can copy the script to the new $HOME/bin/ping_server_from_file.sh file. Within the script, we first test whether the input parameter is a file. We then create an output file with a tile that includes the date. As we enter the loop, we append available servers to this file and list the file at the end of the script:

```
#!/bin/bash
# Author: @theurbanpenguin
# Web: www.theurbapenguin.com
# Script to ping servers from file
# Last Edited: August 2015
if [ ! -f"$1 ] ; then
  echo "The input to $0 should be a filename"
  exit 1
fi
echo "The following servers are up on $(date +%x)"> server.out
done
while read server
do
```

```
    ping -c1 "$server"&& echo "Server up: $server">> server.out
done
cat server.out
```

We can execute the script now in the following manner:

```
$ ping_server_from_file.sh servers.txt
```

The output from the script execution should be similar to the following screenshot:

```
pi@pilabs ~/bin $ ping_server_from_file.sh servers.txt
PING 8.8.8.8 (8.8.8.8) 56(84) bytes of data.
64 bytes from 8.8.8.8: icmp_req=1 ttl=52 time=24.5 ms

--- 8.8.8.8 ping statistics ---
1 packets transmitted, 1 received, 0% packet loss, time 0ms
rtt min/avg/max/mdev = 24.578/24.578/24.578/0.000 ms
PING 8.8.4.4 (8.8.4.4) 56(84) bytes of data.
64 bytes from 8.8.4.4: icmp_req=1 ttl=52 time=24.5 ms

--- 8.8.4.4 ping statistics ---
1 packets transmitted, 1 received, 0% packet loss, time 0ms
rtt min/avg/max/mdev = 24.521/24.521/24.521/0.000 ms
The following servers are up on 29/08/15
Server up: 8.8.8.8
Server up: 8.8.4.4
pi@pilabs ~/bin $ _
```

Creating operator menus

We can provide a menu to the Linux operators who need limited functionality from the shell and do not want to learn the details of command-line use. We can use their login script to launch a menu for them. This menu will provide a list of command selections to choose from. The menu will loop until the user chooses to exit from the menu. We can create a new $HOME/bin/menu.sh script; the basis of the menu loop will be the following:

```
while true
do
......
done
```

The loop we have created here is infinite. The `true` command will always return true and loop continuously; however, we can provide a loop control mechanism to allow the user to leave the menu. To start building the structure of the menu, we will need to echo some text within the loop asking the user for their choice of command. We will clear the screen before the menu is loaded each time and an additional read prompt will appear after the execution of the desired command.

This allows the user to read the output from the command before the screen is cleared and the menu is reloaded. The script will look like the following code at this stage:

```
#!/bin/bash
# Author: @theurbanpenguin
# Web: www.theurbapenguin.com
# Sample menu
# Last Edited: August 2015

while true
do
  clear
  echo "Choose an item: a,b or c"
  echo "a: Backup"
  echo "b: Display Calendar"
  echo "c: Exit"
  read -sn1
  read -n1 -p "Press any key to continue"
done
```

If you execute the script at this stage, there will be no mechanism to leave the script. We have not added any code to the menu selections; however, you can test functionality and exit using the *Ctrl + C* keys.

At this stage, the menu should look similar to the output shown in the following screenshot:

```
Choose an item: a,b or c
a: Backup
b: Display Calendar
c: Exit
```

To build the code behind the menu selection, we will implement a `case` statement. This will be added in between the two `read` commands, as follows:

```
read -sn1
  case "$REPLY" in
    a) tar -czvf $HOME/backup.tgz ${HOME}/bin;;
```

```
     b) cal;;
     c) exit 0;;
esac
read -n1 -p "Press any key to continue"
```

We can see the three options that we have added to the `case` statement, a, b, and c:

- Option a: This runs the `tar` command to back up the scripts
- Option b: This runs the `cal` command to display the current month
- Option c: This exits the script

To ensure that the user is logged out when exiting from their login script, we will run the following:

```
exec menu.sh
```

The `exec` command is used to ensure that the shell is left after the `menu.sh` file is complete. In this way, the user never needs to experience the Linux shell. The complete script is shown in the following screenshot:

```
#!/bin/bash
# Author: @theurbanpenguin
# Web: www.theurbapenguin.com
# Sample menu
# Last Edited: August 2015

while true
do
  clear
  echo "Choose an item: a,b or c"
  echo "a: Backup"
  echo "b: Display Calendar"
  echo "c: Exit"
  read -sn1
  case "$REPLY" in
    a) tar -czvf $HOME/backup.tgz ${HOME}/bin;;
    b) cal;;
    c) exit 0;;
  esac
  read -n1 -p "Press any key to continue"
done
```

Summary

We have begun to make progress within this chapter. We have been able to join many of the elements that we have previously used into cohesive and functional scripts. Although the focus of this chapter has been on loops, we have used command-line lists, if statements, case statements, and arithmetic calculations.

We opened this chapter by describing loops as the workhorse of our scripts and we have been able to demonstrate this with for, while, and until loops. The for loop is used to iterate through elements of a list. The list can be either static or dynamic; with an emphasis on dynamic lists, we showed how simply these are created through file globbing or command expansion.

Also, we saw how to iterate over complex values and how to set the IFS to iterate over fields correctly.

We learned how to write nested loops and how to redirect loop output to files.

The while and until loops are controlled using conditions. The while loop will loop while the supplied condition is true. The until loop will loop until the supplied condition returns true or while it returns false. The continue and break keywords are specific to loops and, using them along with exit, we can control the loop flow.

In the next chapter, we will look at modularizing scripts using functions.

Questions

1. How many lines will be printed on screen from the following script?

```
#!/bin/bash
for (( v1 = 12; v1 <= 34; v1++ ))
do
echo "$v1"
done > output
```

2. How many lines will be printed on the screen from the following script?

```
#!/bin/bash
for (( v=8; v <= 12; v++ ))
do
if [ $v -ge 12 ]
then
break
fi
echo "$v"
done
```

3. What is wrong with the following script? And how can you fix it?

```
#!/bin/bash
for (( v=1, v <= 10, v++ ))
do
echo "value is $v"
done
```

4. How many lines will be printed on the screen from the following script?

```
#!/bin/bash
count=10
while (( count >= 0 )) ; do
echo $count
done
$((count--))
exit 0
```

Further reading

Please see the following for further reading relating to this chapter:

- http://tldp.org/LDP/abs/html/internalvariables.html
- http://tldp.org/HOWTO/Bash-Prog-Intro-HOWTO-7.html
- http://tldp.org/LDP/Bash-Beginners-Guide/html/sect_09_02.html
- http://tldp.org/LDP/Bash-Beginners-Guide/html/sect_09_03.html
- http://tldp.org/LDP/Bash-Beginners-Guide/html/sect_09_05.html

Creating Building Blocks with Functions

7

In this chapter, we will dive into the wonderful world of functions. We can look at these as modular building blocks creating powerful and adaptive scripts. By creating functions, we add the code in a single building block isolated from the rest of the script. Focusing on improvements of a single function is a lot easier than trying to improve the script as a single object. Without functions, it is difficult to hone in on problem areas and the code is often repeated, which means that updates need to happen in many locations. Functions are named as blocks of code or scripts within scripts and they can overcome many problems associated with more complex code.

As we make our way through the chapter, we will cover the following topics:

- Introducing functions
- Passing parameters to functions
- Variable scope
- Returning values from functions
- Recursive functions
- Using functions in menus

Technical requirements

The source code for this chapter can be downloaded from here:

```
https://github.com/PacktPublishing/Mastering-Linux-Shell-Scripting-Second-
Edition/tree/master/Chapter07
```

Introducing functions

Functions are blocks of code that exist in memory as **named elements**. These elements can be created within the shell environment, as well as within the script execution. When a command is issued at the command line, aliases are checked first and, following this, we check for a matching function name. To display the functions residing in your shell environment, you can use the following command:

```
$ declare -F
```

The output will vary depending on the distribution you are using and the number of functions you have created. On my Linux Mint, the partial output is shown in the following screenshot:

Using the small `-f` option, you can display the function and the associated definition. However, if we want to see just a single function definition, we can use the `type` command:

```
$ type quote
```

The previous code example will display the code block for the quote function, if it exists within your shell. We can see the output of this command in the following screenshot:

```
pi@pilabs ~ $ type quote
quote is a function
quote ()
{
    local quoted=${1//\'/\'\\\'\'};
    printf "'%s'" "$quoted"
}
```

The quote function in bash inserts single quotes around a supplied input parameter. For example, we can expand the USER variable and display the value as a string literal; this is shown in the following screenshot. The screenshot captures the command and output:

```
'pi'pi@pilabs ~ $ quote $USER
'pi'pi@pilabs ~ $ _
```

Most code can be represented by a pseudo-code which shows an example layout. Functions are no different and the code to create a function is listed in the following example:

```
function-name() {
<code to execute>
}
```

Also, there is another way of defining functions, like this:

```
function <function-name> {
<code to execute>
}
```

The keyword function is deprecated for portability with the **Portable Operating System Interface (POSIX)** specification, but it is still used by some developers.

Note that the () are not necessary when using the keyword function, but they are a must if you define the function without the keyword function.

The function is created without a do and done block, as we have used in the previous loops. It is the purpose of the curly brackets to define the code block boundaries.

A simple function to display aggregated system information is shown in the following code. This can be created at the command line and will be resident in your shell. This will not persist the logins and will be lost when the shell is closed or the function is unset. To allow the function to persist, we need to add this to the login script of our user account. The sample code is as follows:

```
$ show_system() {
echo "The uptime is:"
uptime
echo
echo "CPU Detail"
lscpu
echo
echo "User list"
who
}
```

We can print the detail of the function similar to the prior instance using the type command; this is shown in the following screenshot:

```
pi@pilabs ~ $ type show_system
show_system is a function
show_system ()
{
    echo "The uptime is:";
    uptime;
    echo;
    echo "CPU Detail";
    lscpu;
    echo;
    echo "User list";
    who
}
```

To execute the function, we simply need to type show_system and we will see the static text and output from the three commands: uptime, lscpu, and who. This is, of course, a very simple function but we can start to add more functionality by allowing parameters to be passed at runtime.

Passing parameters to functions

Earlier within this chapter, we referred to functions as scripts within scripts and we will still maintain that analogy. Similar to how a script can have input parameters, we can create functions that also accept parameters that can make their operation less static. Before we work on a script, we can look at a useful function in the command line.

One of my pet peeves is overcommented configuration files, especially where documentation exists to detail the options available.

The **GNU's Not Unix (GNU)** Linux `sed` command can easily edit the file for us and remove commented lines and empty lines. We are introducing the stream editor, `sed`, here but we will look at it in more detail in the following chapter.

The `sed` command line that runs the in-place edit will be as follows:

```
$ sed -i.bak '/^\s*#/d;/^$/d' <filename>
```

We can run out forensics in the command line by breaking it down element by element. Let's take a deeper look:

- `sed -i.bak`: This edits the file and creates a backup with the extension `.bak`. The original file will then be accessible as `<filename>.bak`.
- `/^`: This caret character (`^`) means edit the lines that start with what after the caret. So the caret matches the beginning of a line.
- `\s*`: This means any amount of white space, including no spaces or tabs.
- `#/`: This is a normal `#` sign. So the total expression `^\s*#` means we are looking for lines that begin with comment or spaces and a comment.
- `d`: This is the delete action to remove matching lines.
- `;/^$/d`: The semicolon is used to separate expressions and the second expression is similar to the first but this time we are preparing to delete empty lines.

To move this into a function, we will simply need to think of a great name. I like to build verbs into function names; it helps with the uniqueness and identifies the purpose of the function. We will create the `clean_file` function as follows:

```
$ function clean_file {
   sed -i.bak '/^\s*#/d;/^$/d' "$1"
}
```

As within scripts, we use positional parameters to accept command-line arguments. We can replace the hardcoded filename that we used previously with $1 within the function. We will quote this variable to protect against spaces within the filename. To test the clean_file function, we will make a copy of a system file and work with the copy. In this way, we can be sure that no harm comes to any system file. We can assure all readers that no system files were harmed during the making of this book. The following are the detailed steps we need to follow to perform the test on the new function:

1. Create the clean_file function as described
2. Move to your home directory using the cd command without arguments
3. Copy the time configuration file to your home directory cp /etc/ntp.conf $HOME
4. Count the number of lines in the file with the following command: wc -l $HOME/ntp.conf
5. Now remove the commented and empty lines with clean_file $HOME/ntp.conf
6. Now recount the lines using wc -l $HOME/ntp.conf
7. Also, check the count the backup of the original file that we created: wc -l $HOME/ntp.conf.bak

The sequence of commands is shown in the following screenshot:

```
likegeeks@likegeeks-VirtualBox ~

File  Edit  View  Search  Terminal  Help

likegeeks@likegeeks-VirtualBox ~/Desktop $ clean_file() {    sed -i.bak '/^\s*#/d;/^$/d' "$1"; }
likegeeks@likegeeks-VirtualBox ~/Desktop $ cd
likegeeks@likegeeks-VirtualBox ~ $ cp /etc/ntp.conf $HOME
likegeeks@likegeeks-VirtualBox ~ $ clean_file $HOME/ntp.conf
likegeeks@likegeeks-VirtualBox ~ $ wc -l $HOME/ntp.conf
15 /home/likegeeks/ntp.conf
likegeeks@likegeeks-VirtualBox ~ $ wc -l $HOME/ntp.conf.bak
66 /home/likegeeks/ntp.conf.bak
likegeeks@likegeeks-VirtualBox ~ $
```

We can direct the attention of the function to the required file using the argument that was supplied while executing the function. If we need to persist this function, then we should add it to a login script. However, if we want to test this within a shell script, we can create the following file to do this and practice some of the other elements we have learned. We will need to take notice that the functions should always be created at the start of the script as they need to be stored in memory by the time they are called. Just think that your function needs to be unlocked and loaded before you pull the trigger.

We will create a new shell script, $HOME/bin/clean.sh, and the execute permission, as always, will need to be set. The code of the script is as follows:

```bash
#!/bin/bash
# Script will prompt for filename
# then remove commented and blank lines

is_file() {
    if [ ! -f "$1" ] ; then
        echo "$1 does not seem to be a file"
        exit 2
    fi
}

clean_file() {
    is_file "$1"
    BEFORE=$(wc -l "$1")
    echo "The file $1 starts with $BEFORE"
    sed -i.bak '/^\s*#/d;/^$/d' "$1"
    AFTER=$(wc -l "$1")
    echo "The file $1 is now $AFTER"
}

read -p "Enter a file to clean: "
clean_file "$REPLY"
exit 1
```

We have provided two functions within the script. The first, is_file, simply tests to ensure that the filename we have entered is a regular file. Then we declare the clean_file function with a little added functionality, displaying the line count of the file before and after the operation. We can also see that functions can be nested and we call the is_file function with clean_file.

Without the function definitions, we have only three lines of code at the end of the file, which we can see in the example code laid out in the previous code block that has been saved as $HOME/bin/clean.sh. We first prompt for the filename and then run the clean_file function, which in turn calls the is_file function. The simplicity of the main code is important here. The complexity is in the functions, as each function can be worked on as a standalone unit.

We can now test the script operation, first using a wrong filename, as we can see in the following screenshot:

```
pi@pilabs ~ $ clean.sh
Enter a file to clean: ntp.cff
ntp.cff does not seem to be a file
pi@pilabs ~ $
```

Now that we have seen the operation with an incorrect file, we can try again using an actual file! We can use the same system file we worked on before. We need to first return the files to their original state:

```
$ cd $HOME
$ rm $HOME/ntp.conf
$ mv ntp.conf.bak ntp.conf
```

With the file now ready, we can execute the script from the $HOME directory as shown in the following screenshot:

```
pi@pilabs ~ $ clean.sh
Enter a file to clean: ntp.conf
The file ntp.conf starts with 55 ntp.conf
The file ntp.conf is now 13 ntp.conf
pi@pilabs ~ $
```

Passing arrays

Not all your passed values will be single values; you may need to pass an array to the function. Let's see how to pass an array as a parameter:

```
#!/bin/bash
myfunc() {
    arr=$@
    echo "The array from inside the function: ${arr[*]}"
}

test_arr=(1 2 3)
echo "The original array is: ${test_arr[*]}"
myfunc ${test_arr[*]}
```

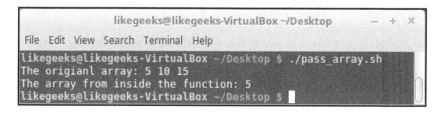

From the result, you can see that the used array is returned the way it is from the function.

Note that we used $@ to get the array inside the function. If you use $1, it will return the first array element only:

```bash
#!/bin/bash
myfunc() {
    arr=$1
    echo "The array from inside the function: ${arr[*]}"
}

my_arr=(5 10 15)
echo "The original array: ${my_arr[*]}"
myfunc ${my_arr[*]}
```

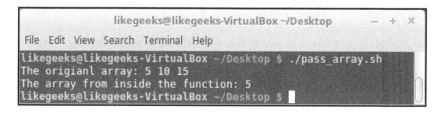

Because we used $1, it returns only the first array element.

Variable scope

By default, any variable you declare inside a function is a global variable. That means this variable can be used outside and inside the function without problems.

Check out this example:

```bash
#!/bin/bash
myvar=10
myfunc() {
    myvar=50
}
```

```
myfunc
echo $myvar
```

If you run this script, it will return 50, which is the value changed inside the function.

What if you want to declare a variable that is exclusive to the function? This is called a local variable.

You can declare local variables by using the `local` command like this:

```
myfunc() {
    local myvar=10
}
```

To ensure that the variable is used only inside the function, let's check out the following example:

```
#!/bin/bash
myvar=30
myfunc() {
    local myvar=10
}
myfunc
echo $myvar
```

If you run this script, it will print 30, which means that the local version of the variable is different than the global version.

Returning values from functions

Whenever we have statements that are printed on the screen within the function, we can see their result. However, lots of times we will want the function to populate a variable within the script and not display anything. In this case, we use `return` in the function. This is especially important when we are gaining input from users. We may prefer the case to translate the input to a known case to make the condition testing easier. Embedding the code in a function allows it to be used many times within a script.

The following code shows how we can achieve this by creating the `to_lower` function:

```
to_lower ()
{
    input="$1"
    output=$( echo $input | tr [A-Z] [a-z])
return $output
}
```

Stepping through the code, we can begin to understand the operation of this function:

- `input="$1"`: This is more for ease than anything else; we assign the first input parameter to a named variable input.
- `output=$( echo $input | tr [A-Z] [a-z])`: This is the main engine of the function, where the translation from uppercase to lowercase occurs. We pipe the input to the `tr` command to convert uppercase to lowercase.
- `return $output`: This is how we create the return value.

One use of this function will be within a script that reads the user's input and simplifies the test to see whether they choose Q or q. This can be seen in the following extract of code:

```
to_lower ()
{
    input="$1"
    output=$( echo $input | tr [A-Z] [a-z])
return $output
}

while true
do
  read -p "Enter c to continue or q to exit: "
  $REPLY=$(to_lower "$REPLY")
  if [ $REPLY = "q" ] ; then
    break
  fi

done
echo "Finished"
```

Recursive functions

A recursive function is a function that calls itself from inside itself. This function is very useful when you need to call the function to do something again from inside of it. The most famous example for that is calculating factorials.

To calculate the factorial of 4, you multiply the number by the descending numbers. You can do it like this:

```
4! = 4*3*2*1
```

The ! sign means factorial.

Let's write a recursive function that calculates the factorial of any given number:

```
#!/bin/bash
calc_factorial() {
if [ $1 -eq 1 ]
then
echo 1
else
local var=$(( $1 - 1 ))
local res=$(calc_factorial $var)
echo $(( $res * $1 ))
fi
}
read -p "Enter a number: " val
factorial=$(calc_factorial $val)
echo "The factorial of $val is: $factorial"
```

First, we define the function which is called `calc_factorial` and inside it we check if the number equals 1 and if so, the function will return 1 because the factorial of 1 equals 1.

Then we decrement the number by one and call the function from inside it and that will call the function again.

This will continue to happen until it reaches 1 and then the function will exit.

Using functions in menus

In Chapter 6, *Iterating with Loops*, we created the `menu.sh` file. Menus are great targets to use functions, as the `case` statement is maintained very simply with single-line entries, while the complexity can still be stored in each function. We should consider creating a function for each menu item. If we copy the previous `$HOME/bin/menu.sh` to `$HOME/bin/menu2.sh`, we can improve the functionality. The new menu should look like the following code:

```bash
#!/bin/bash
# Author: @likegeeks
# Web: likegeeks.com
# Sample menu with functions
# Last Edited: April 2018

to_lower() {
    input="$1"
    output=$( echo $input | tr [A-Z] [a-z])
return $output
}

do_backup() {
    tar -czvf $HOME/backup.tgz ${HOME}/bin
}

show_cal() {
    if [ -x /usr/bin/ncal ] ; then
      command="/usr/bin/ncal -w"
    else
      command="/usr/bin/cal"
    fi
    $command
}

while true
do
```

```
  clear
  echo "Choose an item: a, b or c"
  echo "a: Backup"
  echo "b: Display Calendar"
  echo "c: Exit"
  read -sn1
  REPLY=$(to_lower "$REPLY")
  case "$REPLY" in
    a) do_backup;;
    b) show_cal;;
    c) exit 0;;
  esac
  read -n1 -p "Press any key to continue"
done
```

As we can see, we still maintain the simplicity of the case statement; however, we can develop the script to add in more complexity through the functions. For example, when choosing option b for the calendar, we now check to see whether the ncal command is available. If it is, we use ncal and use the -w option to print the week number. We can see this in the following screenshot, where we have chosen to display the calendar and install ncal:

```
Choose an item: a,b or c
a: Backup
b: Display Calendar
c: Exit
      September 2015
Mo      7 14 21 28
Tu   1  8 15 22 29
We   2  9 16 23 30
Th   3 10 17 24
Fr   4 11 18 25
Sa   5 12 19 26
Su   6 13 20 27
    36 37 38 39 40
Press any key to continue_
```

We can also not be concerned about the *Caps Lock* key as the to_lower function converts our selection to lowercase. Over time, it would be very easy to add additional elements to the functions, knowing that we only affect that single function.

Summary

We are still making progress in leaps and bounds in script writing. I hope these ideas stay with you and you find the code examples useful. Functions are very important for the ease of maintenance of your scripts and their ultimate functionality. The easier the scripts are to maintain, the more likely you are to add improvements over time. We can define functions at the command line or within scripts but they need to be included in the script before they are used.

The functions themselves are loaded into memory while the script is running, but as long as the script is forked and not sourced, they will be released from memory once the script is finished. We have touched a little upon sed in this chapter and we will look more at using the stream editor (sed) in the next chapter. The sed command is very powerful and we can make good use of it within scripts.

Questions

1. What is the printed value of the following code?

```
#!/bin/bash
myfunc() {
arr=$1
echo "The array: ${arr[*]}"
}

my_arr=(1 2 3)
myfunc ${my_arr[*]}
```

2. What is the output of the following code?

```
#!/bin/bash
myvar=50
myfunc() {
myvar=100
}
echo $myvar
myfunc
```

3. What is the problem with the following code? And how can you fix it?

```
clean_file {
    is_file "$1"
    BEFORE=$(wc -l "$1")
    echo "The file $1 starts with $BEFORE"
    sed -i.bak '/^\s*#/d;/^$/d' "$1"
    AFTER=$(wc -l "$1")
    echo "The file $1 is now $AFTER"
}
```

4. What is the problem with the following code? And how can you fix it?

```
#!/bin/bash
myfunc() {
arr=$@
echo "The array from inside the function: ${arr[*]}"
}

test_arr=(1 2 3)
echo "The origianl array is: ${test_arr[*]}"
myfunc (${test_arr[*]})
```

Further reading

Please see the following for further reading relating to this chapter:

- http://tldp.org/HOWTO/Bash-Prog-Intro-HOWTO-8.html
- http://tldp.org/LDP/abs/html/functions.html
- https://likegeeks.com/bash-functions/

Introducing the Stream Editor 8

In the previous chapter, we saw that we could make use of sed to edit files from within our scripts. The sed command is the **stream editor (sed)** and opens the file line by line to search or edit the file content. Historically, this goes way back to Unix, where systems may not have had enough RAM to open very large files. Using sed was absolutely required to carry out edits. Even today, we will use sed to make changes and display data from files with hundreds and thousands of entries. It is simpler and easier and more reliable than a human trying to do the same thing. Most importantly, as we have seen, we can use sed in scripts to edit the files automatically; no human interaction is required.

We will start by looking at grep and searching the files for text. The re in the grep command is short for **regular expression**. Even though we are not looking at scripting in this chapter, we will be covering some very important tools that we can use with scripts. In the next chapter, we will see the practical implementation of sed in scripts.

For the moment though, we have enough to deal with and we will cover the following topics in this chapter:

- Using grep to display text
- Understanding the basics of sed
- Other sed commands
- Multiple sed commands

Technical requirements

The source code for this chapter can be downloaded here:

https://github.com/PacktPublishing/Mastering-Linux-Shell-Scripting-Second-Edition/tree/master/Chapter08

Using grep to display text

We will be beginning this journey by looking at the grep command. This will enable us to grasp some simple concepts of searching through the text before moving onto more complex regular expressions and editing files with sed.

Global regular expression print (grep), or what we more commonly call the grep command, is a command-line tool used to search globally (across all the lines in a file) and print the result to STDOUT. The search string is a regular expression.

The grep command is such a common tool that it has many simple examples and numerous occasions where we can use it each day. In the following sections, we have included some simple and useful examples with explanations.

Displaying received data on an interface

In this example, we will print just the received data from the eth0 interface.

 This is the interface that is my primary network connection. If you are uncertain of your interface name, you can use the ifconfig -a command to display all the interfaces and choose the correct interface name on your system. If ifconfig is not found, try typing the full path, /sbin/ifconfig.

Using just the ifconfig eth0 command, a heap of data can be printed to the screen. To show just the packets received, we can isolate the lines that contain RX packets (RX for received). This is where grep comes in:

```
$ ifconfig eth0 | grep "RX packets"
```

Using the pipe or vertical bars, we can take the output of the ifconfig command and send it to the input of the grep command. In this case, grep is searching for a very simple string, RX packets. The search string is case sensitive, so we need to get this right or use the -i option with grep to run the search as case insensitive, as shown in the following example:

```
$ ifconfig eth0 | grep -i "rx packets"
```

 A case-insensitive search is especially useful when searching for options in a configuration file, which often have mixed cases.

We can see the result of the initial command in the following screenshot, confirming that we have been able to isolate just the single line of output, as shown:

```
pi@pilabs ~ $ ifconfig eth0 | grep "RX packets"
          RX packets:689830 errors:0 dropped:5 overruns:0 frame:0
pi@pilabs ~ $ _
```

Displaying user account data

The local user account database in Linux is the /etc/passwd file and this is readable by all user accounts. If we want to search for the line that contains our own data, we can use either our own login name in the search or use parameter expansion and the $USER variable. We can see this in the following command example:

```
$ grep "$USER" /etc/passwd
```

In this example, the input to grep comes from the /etc/passwd file and we search for the value of the $USER variable. Again, in this case, it is a simple text, but it is still the regular expression, just without any operators.

For completeness, we include the output in the following screenshot:

```
pi@pilabs ~ $ grep "$USER" /etc/passwd
pi:x:1000:1000:,,,:/home/pi:/bin/bash
pi@pilabs ~ $ _
```

We can extend this a little using this type of query as a condition within a script. We can use this to check whether a user account exists before trying to create a new account. To keep the script as simple as possible and to ensure that administrative rights are not required, creating the account will display just the prompt and conditional test in the following command-line example:

```
$ bash
$ read -p "Enter a user name: "
$ if (grep "$REPLY" /etc/passwd > /dev/null) ; then
> echo "The user $REPLY exists"
> exit 1
> fi
```

The grep search now makes use of the $REPLY variable populated by read. If I enter the name pi, a message will be displayed and we will exit because my user account is also called pi. There is no need to display the result from grep; we are just looking for a return code that is either true or false. To ensure that we do not see any unnecessary output if the user is in the file, we redirect the output from grep to the special device file /dev/null.

If you want to run this from the command line, you should start a new bash shell first. You can do this by simply typing bash. In this way, when the exit command runs, it will not log you out but close the newly opened shell. We can see this happening and the results when specifying an existing user in the following screenshot:

```
pi@pilabs ~ $ read -p "Enter a user name: "
Enter a user name: pi
pi@pilabs ~ $ if (grep "$REPLY" /etc/passwd > /dev/null ); then
> echo "The user $REPLY exits"
> exit 1
> fi
The user pi exits
exit
pi@pilabs ~ $ _
```

Listing the number of CPUs in a system

Another really useful feature is that grep can count the matching lines and not display them. We can use this to count the number of CPUs or CPU cores we have on a system. Each core or CPU is listed with a name in the /proc/cpuinfo file. We can then search for the text name and count the output; the -c option used is shown in the following example:

```
$ grep -c name /proc/cpuinfo
```

My CPU has four cores, as shown in the following output:

```
pi@pilabs ~ $ grep -c name /proc/cpuinfo
4
```

If we use the same code on another PC Model B that has a single core, we will see the following output:

```
[pi@black-pearl ~ ]$ grep -c name /proc/cpuinfo
1
[pi@black-pearl ~ ]$
```

We can again make use of this in a script to verify that enough cores are available before running a CPU-intensive task. To test this from the command line, we can use the following code, which we execute on a PC with just a single core:

```
$ bash
$ CPU_CORES=$(grep -c name /proc/cpuinfo)
$ if (( CPU_CORES < 4 )) ; then
> echo "A minimum of 4 cores are required"
> exit 1
> fi
```

We only run `bash` at the start to ensure that we are not logged out of the system with the `exit` command. If this was in a script, this would not be required, as we would exit the script and not our shell session.

By running this on the Model B that has a single core, we can see the results of the script and also the indication that we do not have the required number of cores:

```
[pi@black-pearl ~ ]$ bash
[pi@black-pearl ~ ]$ CPU_CORES=$(grep -c name /proc/cpuinfo)
[pi@black-pearl ~ ]$ if (( CPU_CORES < 4 )); then
> echo "A minumum a 4 cores are required"
> exit 1
> fi
A minumum a 4 cores are required
exit
[pi@black-pearl ~ ]$
```

If you had a requirement to run this check in more than one script, then you could create a function in a shared script and source the script holding the shared functions within the script that needs to be checked:

```
function check_cores {
  [ -z $1 ] && REQ_CORES=2
CPU_CORES=$(grep -c name /proc/cpuinfo)
if (( CPU_CORES < REQ_CORES )) ; then
echo "A minimum of $REQ_CORES cores are required"
exit 1
fi
}
```

If a parameter is passed to the function, then it is used as the required number of cores; otherwise, we set the value to 2 as the default. If we define this as a function in the shell on the Model B PC and display the details with the `type` command, we should see this as shown in the following screenshot:

```
[pi@black-pearl ~ ]$ type check_cores
check_cores is a function
check_cores ()
{
    [ -z $1 ] && REQ_CORES=2;
    CPU_CORES=$(grep -c name /proc/cpuinfo);
    if (( CPU_CORES < REQ_CORES )); then
        echo "A minimum a $REQ_CORES cores are required";
        exit 1;
    fi
}
[pi@black-pearl ~ ]$
```

If we run this on a single-core system and specify the requirement of just a single core, we will see that there is no output when we meet the requirement. If we do not specify the requirement, then it will default to 2 cores and we will fail to meet the requirement and we will exit the shell.

We can see the output of the function when run with the argument of 1, and then without arguments, in the following screenshot:

```
[pi@black-pearl ~ ]$ check_cores 1
[pi@black-pearl ~ ]$ check_cores
A minimum a 2 cores are required
exit
[pi@black-pearl ~ ]$
```

We can see how useful even the basics of `grep` can be within the scripts and how we can use what we have learned to start creating usable modules to add to our scripts.

Parsing CSV files

We will now look at creating a script to parse or format a CSV file. The formatting of the file will add new lines, tabs, and color to the output, so that it is more readable. We can then use `grep` to display single items from the CSV file. The practical application here is a catalog system based on the CSV files.

The CSV file

The CSV file, or list of comma-separated values, will come from the file named `tools` that we have in a current directory. This is a catalog of products that we sell. The file content is shown in the following output:

```
drill,99,5
hammer,10,50
brush,5,100
lamp,25,30
screwdriver,5,23
table-saw,1099,3
```

This is just a simple demonstration, so we don't expect too much data, but each item in the catalog consists of the following:

- Name
- Price
- Units in stock

We can see that we have a drill that costs $99 and we have five units in stock. If we list the file with `cat`, it is not very friendly; however, we can write a script to display the data in a more appealing way. We can create a new script called `$HOME/bin/parsecsv.sh`:

```
#!/bin/bash
OLDIFS="$IFS"
IFS=","
while read product price quantity
do
echo -e "\33[1;33m$product \
        =======================\033[0m\n\
Price : \t $price \n\
```

```
Quantity : \t $quantity \n"

done <"$1"
IFS=$OLDIFS
```

Let's work through this file and look at the pertinent elements:

Element	Meaning
OLDIFS="$IFS"	The IFS variable stores the file separator and this is normally a white space character. We can store the old IFS so that we can restore it later at the end of the script, ensuring that we return the same environment once the script is complete, no matter how the script is run.
IFS=","	We set the separator to a comma to match what we need with a CSV file.
while read product price quantity	We enter a while loop to populate three variables that we need: product, price, and quantity. The while loop will read the input file, line by line, and populate each of the variables.
echo ...	The echo command displays the product name in blue with double underscores underneath. The other variables are printed on new lines and tabbed in.
done <"$1"	This is where we read the input file, which we pass as an argument to the script.

The script is shown in the following screenshot:

```
#!/bin/bash
OLDIFS="$IFS"
IFS=","
while read product price quantity
do
    echo -e "\033[1;34m$product \
    =========================\033[0m\n\
    Price : \t $price \n\
    Quantity : \t $quantity \n"

done < "$1"
IFS=$OLDIFS
```

We can execute the script with the `tools` catalog file located in the current directory using the following command:

```
$ parsecsv.sh tools
```

To look at how this will display, we can view the partial output in the following screenshot:

```
pi@pilabs ~/bin $ parsecsv.sh tools
drill          =========================
        Price :             99
        Quantity :          5

hammer         =========================
        Price :             10
        Quantity :          50

brush          =========================
        Price :             5
```

We are now starting to get the idea that we have a lot of power at the command line to format files in a more readable way and a plain text file does not need to be plain.

Isolating catalog entries

If we need to search for one entry, then we need more than just one line. The entry is in three lines. So, if we search for the hammer, we need to go to the hammer line and the two lines that follow. We do this by using the –A option to `grep`, which is short for after. We need to display the matching line and two lines after. This will be expressed by the following code:

```
$ parsecsv.sh tool | grep -A2 hammer
```

This is displayed in the following screenshot:

```
pi@pilabs ~/bin $ parsecsv.sh tools   | grep -A2 hammer
hammer         =========================
        Price :             10
        Quantity :          50
pi@pilabs ~/bin $
```

Understanding the basics of sed

Having built a little foundation, we can now start to look at some of the operations of sed. The commands will be supplied with most Linux systems and are core commands.

We will dive directly into some simple examples:

```
$ sed 'p' /etc/passwd
```

The p operator will print the matched pattern. In this case, we have not specified a pattern so we will match everything. Printing the matched lines without suppressing STDOUT will duplicate lines. The result of this operation is to print all the lines in the passwd file twice. To print the modified lines only, we use the -n option:

```
$ sed -n 'p' /etc/passwd
```

Brilliant!! We have just reinvented the cat command. We can now specifically work with just a range of lines:

```
$ sed -n '1,3 p ' /etc/passwd
```

Now we have reinvented the head command, but we can also specify the range in a regex pattern to recreate the grep command:

```
$ sed -n '/^root/ p' /etc/passwd
```

We can see this demonstrated in the following screenshot:

```
pi@pilabs ~ $ sed -n '/^root/ p' /etc/passwd
root:x:0:0:root:/root:/bin/bash
pi@pilabs ~ $ _
```

Note that the caret character (^) means the beginning of the line, which means the line must start with the word root. Don't worry; we will explain all these regex characters in a separate chapter.

The substitute command

We have seen the p command for printing the pattern space. The p is actually a flag for the substitute command s.

The substitute command is written like this:

```
$ sed s/pattern/replacement/flags
```

There are three common flags used with the substitute command:

- p: Print the original content
- g: Global replacement for all occurrences
- w: Filename: send results to a file

We will now look at the substitute command or s. With this command, we can replace one string with another. Again, by default, we send the output to the STDOUT and do not edit the file.

To replace the default shell of the user pi, we can use the following command:

```
sed -n ' /^pi/ s/bash/sh/p ' /etc/passwd
```

We continue the earlier instance using the p command to print the matched pattern and use the -n option to suppress STDOUT. We search for lines beginning with pi. This represents the username. We then issue the s command to substitute text in those matched lines. This takes two arguments: the first is the text to search for and the second represents the text used to replace the original. In this case, we look for bash and replace it with sh. This is simple and does work but it may not be reliable in the long term. We can see the output in the following screenshot:

```
pi@pilabs ~ $ sed -n ' /^pi/ s/bash/sh/p ' /etc/passwd
pi:x:1000:1000:,,,:/home/pi:/bin/sh
pi@pilabs ~ $ _
```

We must emphasize that, currently, we are not editing the file and are just displaying it to the screen. The original `passwd` file remains untouched and we can run this as a standard user. I mentioned in the previous example that the search may be less than reliable as the string we are searching for is `bash`. This is very short and perhaps it can be included elsewhere on a matched line. Potentially, someone's last name may be `Tabash`, which includes the string `bash`. We can extend the search to look for `/bin/bash` and replace it with `/bin/sh`. However, this introduces another problem: the default delimiter is the forward slash, so we will have to escape each forward slash we use in the search and replace strings, which is as follows:

```
sed -n ' /^pi/ s/\/bin\/bash/\/usr\/bin\/sh/p ' /etc/passwd
```

This is an option but it is not a tidy option. A better solution is to know that the first delimiter we use defines the delimiters. In other words, you can use any character as a delimiter. Using the @ symbol may be a good idea in this scenario, as it does not appear in either the search or the replace string:

```
sed -n ' /^pi/ s@/bin/bash@/usr/bin/sh@p ' /etc/passwd
```

We now have a more reliable search and a readable command line to work with, which is always a good thing. We replace just the first occurrence on each line of `/bin/bash` with `/bin/sh`. If we need to replace more than the first occurrence, we add the `g` command, for global, at the end:

```
sed -n ' /^pi/ s@bash@sh@pg ' /etc/passwd
```

In our case, it is not required but it is good to know.

Global replacement

Let's assume that we have the following sample file:

```
Hello, sed is a powerful editing tool. I love working with sed
If you master sed, you will be a professional one
```

Let's try to use `sed` against this file:

```
$ sed 's/sed/Linux sed/' myfile
```

Here, we use sed to replace the word sed with Linux sed:

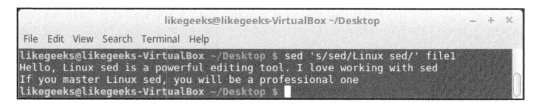

If you check the result carefully, you will notice that sed modified the first word of each line only.

This may not be what you want if you want to replace all occurrences.

Here comes the g flag.

Let's use it and see the results again:

```
$ sed 's/sed/Linux sed/g' myfile
```

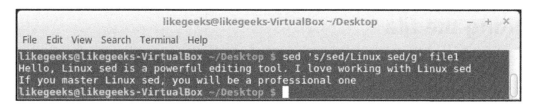

Now all occurrences are modified.

You can port these modifications to a file using the w flag:

```
$ sed 's/sed/Linux sed/w outputfile' myfile
```

Also, you can limit the number of occurrences from the same line, so we can modify the first two occurrences from each line only like this:

```
$ sed 's/sed/Linux sed/2' myfile
```

So, if there is a third occurrence, it will be neglected.

Limiting substitution

We saw how the g flag modifies all occurrences in the same line and this goes for the entire file lines.

What if we want to limit our edits to a specific line? Or a specific line range?

We can specify the ending line or the line range like this:

```
$ sed '2s/old text/new text/' myfile
```

The preceding command will only modify the second line of the file. The following command will modify only the third to the fifth lines:

```
$ sed '3,5s/old text/new text/' myfile
```

The following command will modify from the second line to the end of the file:

```
$ sed '2,$s/old text/new text/' myfile
```

Editing the file

Using the w flag, we can write our edits to a file, but what if we want to edit the file itself? We can use the -i option. We will need permissions to work with the file but we can make a copy of the file to work with, so we don't harm any system file or require additional access.

We can copy the passwd file locally:

```
$ cp /etc/passwd "$HOME"
$ cd
```

We finish with the cd command to ensure that we are working in the home directory and the local passwd file.

The -i option is used to run an in-place update. We will not need the -n option or the p command when editing the file. As such, the command is as simple as the following example:

```
$ sed -i ' /^pi/ s@/bin/bash@/bin/sh/ ' $HOME/passwd
```

There will be no output to the command but the file will now reflect the change. The following screenshot shows the command usage:

```
pi@pilabs ~ $ sed -i ' /^pi/ s@bash@sh@pg ' "$HOME/passwd"
```

We should make a backup before we make the change by appending a string directly after the -i option and without any spaces. This is shown in the following example:

```
$ sed -i.bak ' /^pi/ s@/bin/bash@/bin/sh/ ' $HOME/passwd
```

If we want to see this, we can reverse the search and replace strings:

```
$ sed -i.bak ' /^pi/ s@/bin/sh@/bin/bash/ ' $HOME/passwd
```

This will set the local passwd file to be the same as it was before and we will have a passwd.bak with the previous set of changes. This keeps us safe with a rollback option if we need it.

Other sed commands

sed offers a lot of commands that can be used to insert, change, delete, and transform text with ease. Let's see some examples of how to use these commands with sed.

The delete command

You can use the delete command d to delete lines or a range of lines from your stream. The following command will delete the third line from the stream:

```
$ sed '3d' myfile
```

The following command will delete the third to the fifth line from the stream:

```
$ sed '3,5d' myfile
```

This command will delete from the fourth line to the end of the file:

```
$ sed '4,$d' myfile
```

Note that the deletion happens only to the stream, not the actual file. So if you want to delete from the actual file, you can use the −i option:

```
$ sed −i '2d' myfile #Permenantly delete the second line from the file
```

The insert and append commands

The insert, i, and append, a, commands work the same way with just a slight difference.

The insert command inserts the specified text before the specified line or pattern.

The append command inserts the specified text after the specified line or pattern.

Let's see some examples.

Our sample 02 file will be like this:

```
First line
Second line
Third line
Fourth line
```

To insert a line, you need to use the insert command i like this:

```
$ sed '2i\inserted text' myfile
```

To append a line, you need to use the append command a like this:

```
$ sed '2a\inserted text' myfile
```

Look at the result and check the inserted line position:

The change command

We saw how to substitute occurrences using the substitute command s. So what is the change command and how is it different?

The change command, c, is used for changing the entire line.

To change a line, you can use the change command like this:

```
$ sed '2c\modified the second line' myfile
```

```
                    likegeeks@likegeeks-VirtualBox ~/Desktop          –  +  ×

 File  Edit  View  Search  Terminal  Help

likegeeks@likegeeks-VirtualBox ~/Desktop $ sed '2c\modified the second line' myfile
First line
modified the second line
Third line
Fourth line
likegeeks@likegeeks-VirtualBox ~/Desktop $
```

We replaced the second line with a new line.

The transform command

The transform command is used to replace any letter or a number with another, for example, capitalizing letters or transforming numbers into different numbers.

It works like the tr command.

You can use it like this:

```
$ sed 'y/abc/ABC/' myfile
```

```
                    likegeeks@likegeeks-VirtualBox ~/Desktop          –  +  ×

 File  Edit  View  Search  Terminal  Help

likegeeks@likegeeks-VirtualBox ~/Desktop $ echo 'This is an abc test' | sed 'y/abc/ABC/'
This is An ABC test
likegeeks@likegeeks-VirtualBox ~/Desktop $
```

The transformation applies to the entire stream and can't be limited.

Multiple sed commands

In all the previous examples, we only applied one sed command to our stream. What about running multiple sed commands?

You can do that by using the −e option and separating the commands with a semicolon like this:

```
$ sed -e 's/First/XFirst/; s/Second/XSecond/' myfile
```

Also, you can enter every command on a separate line and you will achieve the same result:

```
$ sed -e '
> s/First/XFirst/
> s/Second/XSecond/' myfile
```

The sed command offers great flexibility; if you use it well, you will gain a lot of power.

Summary

Another great chapter that you have firmly under your belt and I hope it was really useful to you. Although we wanted to concentrate on using sed, we started with how powerful grep can be, both inside and outside our scripts. Although we have only just touched on sed, we will start extending this in the next chapter, where we will expand upon what we have learned.

Also, we learned how to substitute text and how to limit and globalize the substitution and how to save the editing stream using −i.

We learned how to insert, append, delete, and transform text using sed.

Finally, we learned how to run multiple sed commands using the –e option.

In the next chapter, we will learn how to automate Apache Virtual Hosts, how to create new virtual hosts automatically, and other cool stuff. The workhorse of all these operations will be sed and sed scripts.

Questions

1. Suppose you have a file with the following content:

   ```
   Hello, sed is a powerful editing tool. I love working with sed
   If you master sed, you will be a professional one
   ```

   And suppose you use the following command:

   ```
   $ sed 's/Sed/Linux sed/g' myfile
   ```

   How many lines will be substituted?

2. Suppose you have the same file that was used in the previous question and you use the following command:

   ```
   $ sed '2d' myfile
   ```

   How many lines will be deleted from the file?

3. What is the location of the inserted line in the following example?

   ```
   $ sed '3a\Example text' myfile
   ```

4. Suppose you have the same previous sample file and you run the following command:

   ```
   $ sed '2i\inserted text/w outputfile' myfile
   ```

   How many lines will be saved to the output file?

Further reading

Please see the following for further reading relating to this chapter:

- https://www.gnu.org/software/sed/manual/sed.html
- https://linux.die.net/man/1/sed

Automating Apache Virtual Hosts

9

Now that we have seen a little of the **stream editor (sed)**, we can put this knowledge into practice. In Chapter 8, *Introducing the Stream Editor*, we familiarized ourselves with some of the capabilities of sed; however, this represented just a small amount of the power enclosed in the editor. In this chapter, we are going to exercise sed a little more and expose ourselves to some practical uses of the tool, especially when using our bash scripts.

In this journey, we will use sed to help us automate the creation of Apache name-based Virtual Hosts. The Apache hosts are practical users of the sed that we demonstrated but, more importantly, we will use sed to search for selected lines in the main configuration. We will then uncomment those lines and save them as a template. Having created the template, we will create new configurations from it. The concept that we demonstrate with Apache can be applied in many different situations.

We will find that using sed in our shell scripts will allow us to easily extract template data from the main configuration and adjust to the needs of the virtual host. In this way, we will be able to extend the knowledge of both sed and shell scripting. In this chapter, we are going to cover the following topics:

- Apache name-based Virtual Hosts
- Automating virtual host creation

Technical requirements

You will need the following:

- CentOS 7.x machine
- Apache 2.4.x web server installed

You can install Apache as follows:

```
$ sudo yum install httpd
```

Then you can start the web server:

```
$ systemctl start httpd
```

You can ensure that the service is already running by checking the status as follows:

```
$ systemctl status httpd
```

The source code for this chapter can be downloaded from here:

https://github.com/PacktPublishing/Mastering-Linux-Shell-Scripting-Second-Edition/tree/master/Chapter09

Apache name-based Virtual Hosts

For this demonstration, we will be working with the httpd.conf file from an Apache 2.4 HTTPD server taken from a CentOS 7.x host. To be perfectly honest, we are far more interested in the configuration file, as Red Hat or CentOS supply it, than the actual configuration changes that we will make. The file will be available for download from the code bundle of the chapter. Our purpose is to learn how we can extract data from the system-supplied file and create a template from it. We can apply this to Apache configuration files or any other text data file. It is the methodology we are looking at, not the actual result.

To have some understanding of what we are trying to do, we must first look at the `/etc/httpd/conf/httpd.conf` file, that is, CentOS, Red Hat Enterprise Linux, or Scientific Linux. The following screenshot shows the virtual host section of the file that we are interested in:

```
#<VirtualHost *:80>
#     ServerAdmin webmaster@dummy-host.example.com
#     DocumentRoot /www/docs/dummy-host.example.com
#     ServerName dummy-host.example.com
#     ErrorLog logs/dummy-host.example.com-error_log
#     CustomLog logs/dummy-host.example.com-access_log common
#</VirtualHost>
```

Looking at these lines, we can see that they are commented and this is all a part of a monolithic `httpd.conf`. While creating virtual hosts, we normally prefer separate configurations for each of our potential virtual hosts. We need to be able to extract this data from the main file and at the same time uncomment it. We can then save this uncommented data as a template.

Using this template, we will create new configuration files that represent different named `hosts` that we need to have running on one instance of Apache. This enables us to host `sales.example.com` and `marketing.example.com` on a single server. Both sales and marketing will have their own configuration and websites, independent from each other. Additionally, it will also be very easy to add additional sites that we need with the template we create. It becomes the task of the main web server to read the incoming HTTP header requests to the server and direct them to the correct site based on the domain name used.

Our first task then will be to extract the data present between the opening and closing `VirtualHost` tags, uncomment it, and save it to a template. This will only need to be done once and will not be a part of our main script to create the virtual hosts.

Creating the virtual host template

As we are not going to test the virtual hosts we create, we will make a copy of the `httpd.conf` file and work with that locally in our `home` directory. This is good practice while developing the scripts so as not to impact the working configuration. The `httpd.conf` file that I am working with should be able to be downloaded with other script resources referred to in the script from the publisher. Alternatively, you can copy it from your CentOS host with Apache installed. Make sure that the `httpd.conf` file is copied to your `home` directory and that you are working in your `home` directory.

First steps

The very first step in creating the template is to isolate the lines that we need. In our case, this will be the lines included in the sample virtual host definition that we saw in the earlier screenshot. This includes the opening and closing tag for the VirtualHost and everything in between. We can use line numbers for this; however, this will probably not be reliable, as we will need to assume that nothing has changed in the file for the line numbers to be consistent. For completeness, we will show this before moving onto a more reliable mechanism.

First, we will remind ourselves of how we can print the whole file with sed. This is important, as in the next step we will filter the display and show only the lines that we want:

```
$ sed -n ' p ' httpd.conf
```

The -n option is used to suppress the standard output and the sed command within the quotes is p; it is used to display the pattern match. As we have not filtered anything here, the matched pattern is the complete file. If we were to use line numbers to filter, we could add line numbers easily with sed, as shown in the following command:

```
$ sed = httpd.conf
```

From the following screenshot, we can see that, in this system, we need to work with just lines 355 to 361; however, I do stress again that these numbers may vary from file to file:

```
355  #<VirtualHost *:80>
356  #      ServerAdmin webmaster@dummy-host.example.com
357  #      DocumentRoot /www/docs/dummy-host.example.com
358  #      ServerName dummy-host.example.com
359  #      ErrorLog logs/dummy-host.example.com-error_log
360  #      CustomLog logs/dummy-host.example.com-access_log common
361  #</VirtualHost>
362
```

Isolating lines

To display these lines encased with the tags, we can add a number range to sed. This is easily achieved by adding those numbers to sed, as shown in the following command:

```
$ sed -n '355,361 p ' httpd.conf
```

With the range of lines specified, we have been able to easily isolate the lines that we required, and the only lines that are now displayed are those of the virtual host definition. We can see this in the following screenshot, which displays both the command and the output:

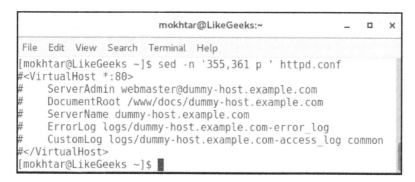

The issue that we face while hardcoding in the line numbers is that we lose flexibility. These line numbers relate to this file and maybe only this file. We will always need to check the correct line numbers in the file that relate to the file we are working with. This could be an issue if the lines are not conveniently at the end of the file and we have to scroll back to try and locate the correct line numbers. To overcome these issues, instead of using line numbers, we can implement a search for the opening and closing tags directly:

```
$ sed -n '/^#<VirtualHost/,/^#<\/VirtualHost/p' httpd.conf
```

We are no longer using the starting number and ending number but the more reliable starting regular expression and closing regular expression. The opening regular expression looks for the line that begins with #<VirtualHost. The ending regular expression is searching for the closing tag. However, we need to protect the /VirtualHost with an escape character. By looking at the end of the regular expression, we see that it translates to lines that begin with #\/VirtualHost, with the escaped forward slash.

If you recall from Chapter 8, *Introducing the Stream Editor*, we specify the lines that begin with a specified character by using the carat (^).

By looking at the following screenshot, we can now isolate the required lines more reliably and without knowing the line numbers. This is more desirable across edited files, which will differ in their line numbering:

```
                              mokhtar@LikeGeeks:~                      _   ▫   ✕

  File  Edit  View  Search  Terminal  Help
[mokhtar@LikeGeeks ~]$ sed -n '/^#<VirtualHost/,/^#<\/VirtualHost/p' httpd.conf
#<VirtualHost *:80>
#     ServerAdmin webmaster@dummy-host.example.com
#     DocumentRoot /www/docs/dummy-host.example.com
#     ServerName dummy-host.example.com
#     ErrorLog logs/dummy-host.example.com-error_log
#     CustomLog logs/dummy-host.example.com-access_log common
#</VirtualHost>
[mokhtar@LikeGeeks ~]$
```

sed script files

Isolating the lines was only the first step! We still have to uncomment the lines and then save the result as a template. Although we can write this as one single `sed` command string, we can already see that it will be awkwardly long and difficult to read and edit. Thankfully, the `sed` command does have the option to read its commands from an input file, often known as a script. We use the `-f` option with `sed` to specify the file we want to read as our control.

We have already seen that we can isolate the correct lines from the file. So, the first line of the script configures the lines that we will work with. We implement the brace brackets `{ }` to define a code block immediately after the selected lines.
A code block is one or more commands that we want to run on a given selection.

In our case, the first command will be to remove the comment and the second command will be to write the pattern space to a new file. The `sed` script should look like the following example:

```
/^#<VirtualHost/,/^#<\/VirtualHost/ {
s/^#//
w template.txt
}
```

We can save this file as $HOME/vh.sed.

In the first line, we select the lines to work with, as we have previously seen, and then open the code block with the left brace. In line 2, we use the substitute command, s. This looks for lines that start with a comment or #. We replace the comment with an empty string. There are no characters or spaces between the middle and end forward slash. In English, we are uncommenting the line but, to the code, this is replacing the # with an empty string. The final line of code uses the write command, w, to save this to template.txt. To help you see this, we have included the following screenshot of the vh.sed file:

```
/^#<VirtualHost/,/^#<\/VirtualHost/ {
s/^#//
w template.txt
}
```

We can see all of our efforts come to fruition now by ensuring that we are in the same directory as the httpd.conf and vh.sed files that are executing the following command:

```
$ sed -nf vh.sed httpd.conf
```

We have now created the template.txt file within our working directory. This is the isolated uncommented text from the httpd.conf file. In simple terms, we have extracted the seven correct lines from over 350 lines of text in milliseconds, removed the comment, and saved the result as a new file. The template.txt file is displayed in the following screenshot:

```
mokhtar@LikeGeeks:~
File  Edit  View  Search  Terminal  Help
[mokhtar@LikeGeeks ~]$ cat template.txt
<VirtualHost *:80>
    ServerAdmin webmaster@dummy-host.example.com
    DocumentRoot /www/docs/dummy-host.example.com
    ServerName dummy-host.example.com
    ErrorLog logs/dummy-host.example.com-error_log
    CustomLog logs/dummy-host.example.com-access_log common
</VirtualHost>
[mokhtar@LikeGeeks ~]$
```

Now we have a template file that we can begin to work with to create virtual host definitions. Even though it's Apache that we have been looking at, the same idea of uncommenting the text or removing the first character of selected lines can apply to many situations, so take this as an idea of what sed can do.

Automating virtual host creation

After having created the template, we can now use this to create virtual host configurations. In the simplest terms, we need to replace the dummy-host.example.com URL with the sales.example.com or marketing.example.com URL. Of course, we have to also create the DocumentRoot directory, the directory where the web pages will be, and also add some basic content. When we use a script to run through the process, nothing will be forgotten and the edits will be accurate every time. The basics of the script will be as follows:

```
#!/bin/bash
WEBDIR=/www/docs
CONFDIR=/etc/httpd/conf.d
TEMPLATE=$HOME/template.txt
[ -d $CONFDIR ] || mkdir -p $CONFDIR
sed s/dummy-host.example.com/$1/ $TEMPLATE > $CONFDIR/$1.conf
mkdir -p $WEBDIR/$1
echo "New site for $1" > $WEBDIR/$1/index.html
```

We can ignore the shebang in the first line; we should know this by now. We can start our explanation on line 2 of the script:

Line	Meaning
WEBDIR=/www/docs/	We initialize the WEDIR variable that we store in the path to the directory that will hold the different websites.
CONFDIR=/etc/httpd/conf.d	We initialize the CONFDIR variable that we will use to store the newly created virtual host configuration file.
TEMPLATE=$HOME/template.txt	We initialize the variable that we will use for the template. This should point to the path of our template.
[-d $CONFDIR] \|\| mkdir -p "$CONFDIR"	On a working EL6 host, this directory will exist and is included in the main configuration. If we are running this as a pure test, then we can create a directory to prove that we can create the correct configuration within the target directory.

`sed s/dummy-host.example.com/$1/ $TEMPLATE >$CONFDIR/$1.conf`	The `sed` command works as an engine in the script, running the search and replace operations. Using the substitute command in `sed`, we search for the dummy text and replace it with the argument passed to the script.
`mkdir -p $WEBDIR/$1`	Here, we create the correct subdirectory to house the websites for the new virtual host.
`echo "New site for $1" > $WEBDIR/$1/index.html`	In this final step, we create a basic holding page for the website.

We can create this script as `$HOME/bin/vhost.sh`. Don't forget to add the execute permission. This is illustrated in the following screenshot:

```
mokhtar@LikeGeeks:~
File  Edit  View  Search  Terminal  Help
[mokhtar@LikeGeeks ~]$ cat vhost.sh
#!/bin/bash
WEBDIR=/www/docs
CONFDIR=/etc/httpd/conf.d
TEMPLATE=$HOME/template.txt
[ -d $CONFDIR ] || mkdir -p $CONFDIR
sed s/dummy-host.example.com/$1/ $TEMPLATE > $CONFDIR/$1.conf
mkdir -p $WEBDIR/$1
echo "New site for $1" > $WEBDIR/$1/index.html
[mokhtar@LikeGeeks ~]$
```

To create the sales virtual host and web page, we can run the script as shown in the following example. We will be running the script directly as the root user. Alternatively, you may choose to make use of the `sudo` command within the script:

```
# vhost.sh sales.example.com
```

We can now see how easily we can create virtual hosts using a well-crafted script. The configuration file for the virtual host will be created in the `/etc/httpd/conf.d/` directory and will be named `sales.example.com.conf`. The file will look similar to the following screenshot:

```
                          mokhtar@LikeGeeks:~

 File  Edit  View  Search  Terminal  Help
[mokhtar@LikeGeeks ~]$ cat /etc/httpd/conf.d/sales.example.com.conf
<VirtualHost *:80>
    ServerAdmin webmaster@sales.example.com
    DocumentRoot /www/docs/sales.example.com
    ServerName sales.example.com
    ErrorLog logs/sales.example.com-error_log
    CustomLog logs/sales.example.com-access_log common
</VirtualHost>
[mokhtar@LikeGeeks ~]$ █
```

The website content must have been created in the `/www/docs/sales.example.com` directory. This will be a simple holding page that proves the point that we can do this from the script. Using the following command, we can list the content or the base directory that we use to house each site:

```
$ ls -R /www/docs
```

The `-R` option allows for the recursive listing. We have used the `/www/docs` directory purely as this is set in the original virtual host definition that we extracted. You may prefer to use `/var/www` or something similar if working in a live environment rather than creating the new directory at the root of your filesystem. It would be a simple matter of editing the template that we created and that too could be done with `sed` at the time of template creation.

Prompting for data during site creation

We can now use the script to create the virtual hosts and the content but we have not allowed for any customization other than the virtual hostname. Of course, this is important. After all, it is this virtual hostname that is used in the configuration itself as well as in setting the website directory and the configuration file name.

It is possible that we could allow additional options to be specified during the virtual host creation. We will use `sed` to insert the data as required. The `sed` command `i` is used to insert data before the selection and `a` to append after the selection.

For our example, we will add a host restriction to allow only the local network access to the website. We are more interested in inserting data into the file rather than what we are doing with the specific HTTP configuration file. Within the script, we will be adding read prompts and inserting a Directory block into the configuration.

To try and explain what we are trying to do, we should see something similar to the following when executing the script. You can see from the text that we are creating this for the marketing site and adding in restrictions as to who can access the site:

```
[root@apache bin]# ./vhost2.sh marketing.example.com
Do you want to restrict access to this site? y/n y
Which network should we restrict access to: 192.168.0.0/24
[root@apache bin]#
```

As you can see, we can ask two questions but, if needed, more of them can be added to support customization, the idea being that the additional customization should be accurate and reliable in the same way as the script creation was. You may also choose to elaborate the questions with sample answers, so that the user knows how the network address should be formatted.

To aide script creation, we will copy the original vhost.sh to vhost2.sh. We can tidy up a few items in the script to allow for easier expansion and then add in the additional prompts. The new script will look similar to the following code:

```
#!/bin/bash
WEBDIR=/www/docs/$1
CONFDIR=/etc/httpd/conf.d
CONFFILE=$CONFDIR/$1.conf
TEMPLATE=$HOME/template.txt
[ -d $CONFDIR ] || mkdir -p $CONFDIR
sed s/dummy-host.example.com/$1/ $TEMPLATE > $CONFFILE
mkdir -p $WEBDIR
echo "New site for $1" > $WEBDIR/index.html
read -p "Do you want to restrict access to this site? y/n "
[ ${REPLY^^} = 'n' ] && exit 0
read -p "Which network should we restrict access to: " NETWORK
sed -i "/<\/VirtualHost>/i <Directory $WEBDIR >\
  \n  Order allow,deny\
  \n  Allow from 127.0.0.1\
  \n  Allow from $NETWORK\
\n</Directory>" $CONFFILE
```

Please note that we are not running too many checks in the script. This is to keep our focus on the elements that we are adding rather than a robust script. In your own environment, once you have the script working the way you want, you may need to implement more checks to ensure script reliability.

As you can see, we have a few more lines. The WEBDIR variable has been adjusted to contain the full path to the directory and, in a similar way, we have added a new variable CONFFILE, so that we can make a reference to the file directly. If the answer to the first prompt is n and the user wants no additional customization, the script will exit. If they answer anything other than n for no, the script will continue and prompt the network to grant access. We can then use sed to edit the existing configuration and insert the new directory block. This will default to deny access but allow access from the localhost and NETWORK variables. We refer to the localhost as 127.0.0.1 in the code.

To simplify the code for better understanding, the pseudo-code will look like the following example:

```
$ sed -i "/SearchText/i NewText <filename>
```

Here SearchText represents the line in the file before which we want to insert our text. Also, NewText represents the new line or lines that will be added before the SearchText. The i command directly following the SearchText dictates that we are inserting text. Using the a command to append will mean that the text we add will be added after the SearchText.

We can see the resulting configuration file for marketing.example.com, as we have created it with the additional Directory block added in the following screenshot:

```
[root@apache bin]# cat /etc/httpd/conf.d/marketing.example.com.conf
<VirtualHost *:80>
    ServerAdmin webmaster@marketing.example.com
    DocumentRoot /www/docs/marketing.example.com
    ServerName marketing.example.com
    ErrorLog logs/marketing.example.com-error_log
    CustomLog logs/marketing.example.com-access_log common
<Directory /www/docs/marketing.example.com >
  Order allow,deny
  Allow from 127.0.0.1
  Allow from 192.168.0.0/24
</Directory>
</VirtualHost>
```

We can see that we have added the new block above the closing `VirtualHost` tag. In the script, this is the `SearchText` that we use. The `Directory` block we add replaces the `NewText` in the pseudo-code. When we look at it, it appears more complex as we have embedded the new lines with \n and formatted the file for easier reading with the line continuation character \. Again, we have to emphasize that this edit is easy and accurate once the script is created.

For completeness, we include the following screenshot of the script `vhost2.sh`:

```
[root@apache bin]# cat vhost2.sh
#!/bin/bash
WEBDIR=/www/docs/$1
CONFDIR=/etc/httpd/conf.d
CONFFILE=$CONFDIR/$1.conf
TEMPLATE=$HOME/template.txt
[ -d $CONFDIR ] || mkdir -p $CONFDIR
sed s/dummy-host.example.com/$1/ $TEMPLATE > $CONFFILE
mkdir -p $WEBDIR
echo "New site for $1" > $WEBDIR/index.html
read -p "Do you want to restrict access to this site? y/n "
[ $REPLY = 'n' ] && exit 0
read -p "Which network should we restrict access to: " NETWORK
sed -i "/<\/VirtualHost>/i <Directory $WEBDIR >\
   \n  Order allow,deny\
   \n  Allow from 127.0.0.1\
   \n  Allow from $NETWORK\
\n</Directory>" $CONFFILE
```

Summary

In this chapter, we have seen how we can extend `sed` into some very cool scripts that have allowed us to extract data from files, uncomment selected lines, and write new configurations. Not stopping at that, we also saw how we could use `sed` with script that inserts new lines into existing files. I think that `sed` will very quickly become your friend and we have created some powerful scripts to support the learning experience.

You may already know this but `sed` has a big brother, `awk`. In the next chapter, we are going to see how we can use `awk` to extract data from files.

Questions

1. How can you print line number 50 from an Apache configuration file?
2. How can you change the Apache default port 80 to 8080 using `sed`?

Further reading

Please see the following for further reading relating to this chapter:

- `https://httpd.apache.org/docs/2.2/`
- `https://httpd.apache.org/docs/2.2/vhosts/examples.html`

10
AWK Fundamentals

The stream editor is not alone in its family and has a big brother, AWK. In this chapter, we will run through the basics of AWK and explore the power of the AWK programming language. We will learn why we need and love AWK and how we can make use of some of the basic features before we start putting AWK to practical use in the next two chapters. As we work our way through this, we will cover the following topics:

- The history behind AWK
- Displaying and filtering content from files
- AWK variables
- Conditional statements
- Formatting output
- Further filtering to display users by UID
- AWK control files

Technical requirements

The source code for this chapter can be downloaded here:

```
https://github.com/PacktPublishing/Mastering-Linux-Shell-Scripting-Second-
Edition/tree/master/Chapter10
```

The history behind AWK

The `awk` command is a command suite mainstay in both UNIX and Linux. The UNIX `awk` command was first developed by Bell Labs in the 1970s and is named after the surnames of the main authors: Alfred Aho, Peter Weinberger, and Brian Kernighan. The `awk` command allows access to the AWK programming language, which is designed to process data within text streams.

There are many implementations of AWK:

- **gawk**: Also known as GNU AWK, it is a free version of AWK and used by many developers; we will use it in this book.
- **mawk**: Another implementation made by a guy named Mike Brennan. This implementation only includes a few gawk features; it was designed for speed and performance.
- **tawk**: Or Thompson AWK, is an implementation that works on Solaris, DOS, and Windows.
- **BWK awk**: Also known as nawk, it is used by OpenBSD and macOS.

Note that the `awk` interpreter that we will use in this book is `gawk` but there is a symbolic link for it with the name `awk`. So `awk` and `gawk` are the same command.

You can ensure this by listing the `awk` binary to see where it points to:

To demonstrate the programming language that is provided with `awk`, we should create a `Hello World` program. We know this is compulsory for all languages:

```
$ awk 'BEGIN { print "Hello World!" }'
```

Not only can we see that this code will print the ubiquitous hello message, we can also generate header information with the `BEGIN` block. Later, we will see that we can create summary information with an `END` code block by allowing for a main code block.

We can see the output of this basic command in the following screenshot:

```
pi@pilabs ~ $ awk ' BEGIN { print "Hello World!" } '
Hello World!
pi@pilabs ~ $ _
```

Displaying and filtering content from files

Now, of course we all want to be able to print a little more than just Hello World. The awk command can be used to filter content from files and, if needed, very large files. We should begin by printing the complete file before filtering it. In this way, we will get a feel for the syntax of the command. Later, we will see how we can add this control information into awk files to ease the command line. Using the following command, we will print all the lines from the /etc/passwd file:

```
$ awk ' { print } ' /etc/passwd
```

This is equivalent to using the $0 variable with the print statement:

```
$ awk ' { print $0 }' /etc/passwd
```

AWK provides us with some ready-to-use variables to extract data such as:

- $0 for the entire line
- $1 for the first field
- $2 for the second field
- $3 for the third field and so on

However, we will need to specify that in this file the field separator used is a colon, since it's the field separator in /etc/passwd file. The awk default delimiter is a space or any amount of spaces or tabs and newlines. There are two ways to specify the input delimiter; these are displayed in the following examples.

The first example is easy and simple to use. The -F option works well, especially where we do not need any additional header information:

```
$ awk -F":" '{ print $1 }' /etc/passwd
```

We could also do this within the BEGIN block; this is useful when we want to use the BEGIN block to display header information:

```
$ awk ' BEGIN { FS=":" } { print $1 } ' /etc/passwd
```

We can see this clearly in the preceding example, in which we named the BEGIN block and all of the code within it is corralled by the brace brackets. The main block has no name and is enclosed within the brace brackets.

After seeing the BEGIN block and the main code blocks, we will now look at the END code block. This is often used to display summary data. For example, if we want to print the total lines in the passwd file, we can make use of the END block. The code with the BEGIN and END blocks is processed just once, whereas the main block is processed for each line. The following example adds to the code we have written so far to include the total line count:

```
$ awk ' BEGIN { FS=":" } { print $1 } END { print NR } ' /etc/passwd
```

The awk internal variable NR maintains the number of processed lines. If we want, we can add some additional text to this. This can be used to annotate the summary data. We can also make use of the single quotes that are used with the AWK language; they will allow us to spread the code across multiple lines. Once we have opened the single quotes, we can add newlines to the command line right until we close the quote. This is demonstrated in the next example where we have extended the summary information:

```
$ awk ' BEGIN { FS=":" }
> { print $1 }
> END { print "Total:",NR } ' /etc/passwd
```

If we do not wish to end our AWK experience here, we can easily display a running line count with each line, as well as the final total. This is shown in the following example:

```
$ awk ' BEGIN { FS=":" }
> { print NR,$1 }
> END { print "Total:",NR } ' /etc/passwd
```

The following screenshot captures this command and shows a partial output:

```
pi@pilabs ~ $ awk ' BEGIN { FS=":" }
{ print NR,$1 }
END { print "Total:",NR } ' /etc/passwd
1 root
2 daemon
3 bin
4 sys
5 sync
```

In the first example with BEGIN, we saw that there is no reason why we cannot use the END code block in isolation without a main code block. If we need to emulate the wc -l command, we can use the following awk statement:

```
$ awk ' END { print NR }' /etc/passwd
```

The output will be the line count from the file. The following screenshot shows both the use of the awk command and the wc command to count the lines in the /etc/passwd file:

```
pi@pilabs ~ $ awk ' END { print NR } ' /etc/passwd
28
pi@pilabs ~ $ wc -l /etc/passwd
28 /etc/passwd
```

As we can see, the output does tally with 28 lines and our code has worked.

Another feature that we can practice with is working on selected lines only. For example, if we want to print only the first five lines, we will use the following statement:

```
$ awk ' NR < 6 ' /etc/passwd
```

If we want to print lines 8 through to 12, we can use the following code:

```
$ awk ' NR==8,NR==12 ' /etc/passwd
```

We can also use regular expressions to match the text in the lines. Take a look at the following example where we look at the lines that end in the word bash:

```
$ awk ' /bash$/ ' /etc/passwd
```

The example and the output it produces are shown in the following screenshot:

```
pi@pilabs ~ $ awk '/bash$/ ' /etc/passwd
root:x:0:0:root:/root:/bin/bash
pi:x:1000:1000:,,,:/home/pi:/bin/bash
bob:x:1001:1004::/home/bob:/bin/bash
joe:x:1002:1005::/home/joe:/bin/bash
pi@pilabs ~ $ _
```

So if you want to use a regex pattern, you should use two slashes and write the pattern between them, /bash$/.

AWK variables

We saw how to use data fields such as $1 and $2. Also, we saw the NR field, which holds the number of processed lines, but there are more built-in variables that AWK offers to simplify work more and more.

- FIELDWIDTHS: Specifies the field width
- RS: Specifies the record separator
- FS: Specifies the field separator
- OFS: Specifies the output separator, which is a space by default
- ORS: Specifies the output separator
- FILENAME: Holds the processed file name
- NF: Holds the line being processed
- FNR: Holds the record which is processed
- IGNORECASE: Ignores character case

These variables can help you a lot in many cases. Let's assume that we have the following file:

```
John Doe
15 back street
(123) 455-3584
Mokhtar Ebrahim
10 Museum street
(456) 352-3541
```

We can say that we have two records for two persons and each record contains three fields. Let's assume that we need to print the name and the phone number. So how do we make AWK process them correctly?

In this case, the fields are separated by a newline (\n) and the records are separated by empty lines.

So if we set the FS to (\n) and the RS to empty text, the fields will be identified correctly:

```
$ awk 'BEGIN{FS="\n"; RS=""} {print $1,$3}' myfile
```

```
likegeeks@likegeeks-VirtualBox ~/Desktop
File Edit View Search Terminal Help
likegeeks@likegeeks-VirtualBox ~/Desktop $ awk 'BEGIN{FS="\n"; RS=""} {print $1,$3}' myfile
John Doe (123) 455-3584
Mokhtar Ebrahim (456) 352-3541
likegeeks@likegeeks-VirtualBox ~/Desktop $ 
```

The result appears valid and appropriate.

In the same way, you can use the OFS and ORS for the output report:

```
$ awk 'BEGIN{FS="\n"; RS=""; OFS="*"} {print $1,$3}' myfile
```

```
likegeeks@likegeeks-VirtualBox ~/Desktop
File Edit View Search Terminal Help
likegeeks@likegeeks-VirtualBox ~/Desktop $ awk 'BEGIN{FS="\n"; RS=""; OFS="*"} {print $1,$3}' myfile
John Doe*(123) 455-3584
Mokhtar Ebrahim*(456) 352-3541
likegeeks@likegeeks-VirtualBox ~/Desktop $ 
```

You can use any text that fits your needs.

We know that NR holds the number of the processed line and FNR looks the same from the definition, but let's explore the following example to see the difference:

Assume that we have the following file:

```
Welcome to AWK programming
This is a test line
And this is one more
```

Let's process this file using AWK:

```
$ awk 'BEGIN{FS="\n"}{print $1,"FNR="FNR}' myfile myfile
```

```
likegeeks@likegeeks-VirtualBox ~/Desktop
File Edit View Search Terminal Help
likegeeks@likegeeks-VirtualBox ~/Desktop $ awk 'BEGIN{FS=","}{print $1,"FNR="FNR}' myfile myfile
Welcome to AWK programming FNR=1
This is a test line FNR=2
And this is one more FNR=3
Welcome to AWK programming FNR=1
This is a test line FNR=2
And this is one more FNR=3
likegeeks@likegeeks-VirtualBox ~/Desktop $ 
```

Here we processed the file twice for testing purposes only to see what the value of the FNR variable is.

As you can see, the value starts from 1 for every processing cycle.

Let's see the whether NR variable is used in the same way:

```
$ awk 'BEGIN {FS="\n"} {print $1,"FNR="FNR,"NR="NR} END{print "Total lines:
",NR}' myfile myfile
```

The NR variable preserves its value during the entire processing while FNR started from 1.

User-defined variables

You can define your own variables to use in AWK programming, as with any programming language.

You can define the variable using any text, but it **MUST** not start with numbers:

```
$ awk '
BEGIN{
var="Welcome to AWk programming"
print var
}'
```

You can define any type of variables and use it the same way.

You can define numbers like this:

```
$ awk '
BEGIN{
var1=2
var2=3
var3=var1+var2
print var3
}'
```

Or perform string concatenation like this:

```
$ awk '
BEGIN{
str1="Welcome "
str2=" To shell scripting"
str3=str1 str2
print str3
}'
```

As you can see, AWK is a powerful scripting language.

Conditional statements

AWK supports conditional statements such as `if` and `while` loops.

The if command

Assume you have the following file:

```
50
30
80
70
20
90
```

Now, let's filter the values:

```
$ awk '{if ($1 > 50) print $1}' myfile
```

The `if` statement checks every value and, if it's greater than 50, it will print it.

You can use `else` clauses like this:

```
$ awk '{
if ($1 > 50)
{
x = $1 * 2
print x
} else
{
x = $1 * 3
print x
}}' myfile
```

```
                        likegeeks@likegeeks-VirtualBox ~/Desktop
 File  Edit  View  Search  Terminal  Help
likegeeks@likegeeks-VirtualBox ~/Desktop $ awk '{
> if ($1 > 50)
> {
> x = $1 * 2
> print x
> } else
> {
> x = $1 * 3
> print x
> }}' myfile
150
90
160
140
60
180
likegeeks@likegeeks-VirtualBox ~/Desktop $
```

If you don't use brackets { } to enclose your statements, you can type them on the same line with a semicolon:

```
$ awk '{if ($1 > 50) print $1 * 2;  else print $1 * 3}' myfile
```

 Note that you can save this code into a file and assign it to the awk command using the -f option, as we will see later on this chapter.

while loops

AWK processes every line of your file, but what if you want to iterate over the fields of each line itself?

You can iterate over fields using a while loop when using AWK.

Assume we have the following file:

```
321  524  124
174  185  254
195  273  345
```

Now let's iterate over the fields using a `while` loop.

```
$ awk '{
total = 0
i = 1
while (i < 4)
{
total += $i
i++
}
mean = total / 3
print "Mean value:",mean
}' myfile
```

The `while` loop iterates over the fields; we get the mean value for every row and print it.

for loops

You can use `for` loops to iterate over values when using AWK like this:

```
$ awk '{
total = 0
for (var = 1; var < 4; var++)
{
total += $var
}
mean = total / 3
print "Mean value:",mean
}' myfile
```

```
                    osboxes@osboxes ~/Desktop
  File  Edit  View  Search  Terminal  Help
osboxes@osboxes ~/Desktop $ awk '{
> total = 0
> for (var = 1; var < 4; var++)
> {
> total += $var
> }
> mean = total / 3
> print "Mean value:",mean
> }' myfile
Mean value: 323
Mean value: 204.333
Mean value: 271
osboxes@osboxes ~/Desktop $ █
```

We achieved the same result but using the `for` loop this time.

Formatting output

We have remained faithful to the `print` command so far, as we have been limited in what we require from the output. If we want to print out, say, the username, UID, and default shell, we need to start formatting the output just a little. In this case, we can organize the output in well-shaped columns. Without formatting, the command we use will look similar to the following example, where we use commas to separate the field that we want to print:

```
$ awk ' BEGIN { FS=":" } { print $1,$3,$7 } ' /etc/passwd
```

We use the BEGIN block here, as we can make use of it to print column headers later.

To understand the problem a little better, take a look at the following screenshot, which illustrates uneven column widths:

```
pi@pilabs ~ $ awk ' BEGIN { FS=":" } { print $1,$3,$7 } ' /etc/passwd
root 0 /bin/bash
daemon 1 /bin/sh
bin 2 /bin/sh
sys 3 /bin/sh
sync 4 /bin/sync
```

The issue that we have in the output is that the columns do not align, as the username is an inconsistent length. To improve on this, we can use the printf function where we can specify the column width. The syntax for the awk statements will be similar to the following example:

```
$ awk ' BEGIN { FS=":" }
> { printf "%10s %4d %17s\n",$1,$3,$7 } ' /etc/passwd
```

The printf formatting is included within double quotes. We also need to include the newline with the \n. The printf function does not add a newline automatically, whereas the print function does. We print the three fields; the first accepts string values and is set to 10 characters wide. The middle field accepts up to 4 numbers and we finish with the default shell field where we allow up to 17 string characters.

The following screenshot shows how the output can be improved:

```
pi@pilabs ~ $ awk ' BEGIN { FS=":" }
{ printf "%10s %4d %17s\n",$1,$3,$7 } ' /etc/passwd
      root    0        /bin/bash
    daemon    1          /bin/sh
       bin    2          /bin/sh
       sys    3          /bin/sh
      sync    4        /bin/sync
     games    5          /bin/sh
       man    6          /bin/sh
```

We can further enhance this by adding header information. Although the code starts to look untidy at this stage, we will later see how we can resolve this with AWK control files. The following example shows the header information being added to the Begin block. The semicolon is used to separate the two statements in the BEGIN block:

```
$ awk 'BEGIN {FS=":" ;printf "%10s %4s %17s\n","Name","UID","Shell" }
> { printf "%10s %4d %17s\n",$1,$3,$7 } ' /etc/passwd
```

In the following screenshot, we can see how this improves the output even further:

```
pi@pilabs ~ $ awk 'BEGIN {FS=":";printf "%10s %4s %17s\n","Name","UID","Shell" }

{ printf "%10s %4d %17s\n",$1,$3,$7 } ' /etc/passwd
      Name  UID            Shell
      root    0        /bin/bash
    daemon    1          /bin/sh
       bin    2          /bin/sh
       sys    3          /bin/sh
```

In the previous chapter, we saw how we can augment the output with the use of colors in the shell. We may also use color from within AWK by adding our own functions. In the next code example, you will see that AWK allows us to define our own functions to facilitate more complex operations and isolate the code. We will now modify the previous code to include green output in the header:

```
$ awk 'function green(s) {
> printf "\033[1;32m" s "\033[0m\n"
> }
> BEGIN {FS=":";
green("    Name:   UID:     Shell:") }
> { printf "%10s %4d %17s\n",$1,$3,$7 } ' /etc/passwd
```

Creating the function within `awk` allows color to be added where we require, in this case, green text. It is easy to create functions to define other colors. The code and output are included in the following screenshot:

```
pi@pilabs ~ $ awk 'function green(s) {
printf "\033[1;32m" s "\033[0m\n"
}
BEGIN {FS=":";
green("    Name:   UID:     Shell:") }
{ printf "%10s %4d %17s\n",$1,$3,$7 } ' /etc/passwd

      root    0           /bin/bash
    daemon    1            /bin/sh
       bin    2            /bin/sh
       sys    3            /bin/sh
```

Further filtering to display users by UID

We have been able to build our skills with AWK, piece by piece, and what we have learned has been useful. We can take these tiny steps and add them to start creating something a little more usable. Perhaps we want to print just standard users; these are usually users higher than 500 or 1,000 depending on your particular distribution.

On the Linux Mint distribution that I am using for this book, standard users start with UID `1000`. The UID is the third field. This is really a simple matter of using the value of the third field as the range operator. We can see this in the following example:

```
$ awk -F":" '$3 > 999 ' /etc/passwd
```

We can show users whose UID is `101` or lower with the following command:

```
$ awk -F":" '$3 < 101 ' /etc/passwd
```

These just give you an idea of some of the possibilities available with AWK. The reality is that we can play all day with our arithmetic comparison operators.

We have also seen that, with some of these examples, the awk statements become a little long. This is where we can implement the awk control files. Let's take a look at these straightaway before we get lost in a morass of syntax.

AWK control files

Just as with sed, we can simplify the command line by creating and including control files. This also makes editing the command later more easily achievable. The control files contain all the statements that we want awk to execute. The main thing that we must consider with sed, awk, and shell scripts is modularization; creating reusable elements that can be used to isolate and reuse the codes. This saves us time and work and we get more time for the tasks that we enjoy.

To see an example of an awk control file, we should revisit the formatting of the passwd file. Creating the following file will encapsulate the awk statements:

```
function green(s) {
    printf "\033[1;32m" s "\033[0m\n"
}
BEGIN {
    FS=":"
    green("   Name:   UID:       Shell:")
}
{
    printf "%10s %4d %17s\n",$1,$3,$7
}
```

We can save this file as `passwd.awk`.

Being able to encompass all awk statements in the one file is very convenient and the execution becomes clean and tidy:

```
$ awk -f passwd.awk /etc/passwd
```

This certainly encourages more complex awk statements and allows you to extend more functionality to your code.

Built-in functions

In the previous example, we defined a function called green. This leads into taking about some built-in functions that come with awk.

AWK comes with many built-in functions such as mathematical functions:

- sin(x)
- cos(x)
- sqrt(x)
- exp(x)
- log(x)
- rand()

You can use them like this:

```
$ awk 'BEGIN{x=sqrt(5); print x}'
```

Also, there are built-in functions that can be used in string manipulation:

```
$ awk 'BEGIN{x = "welcome"; print toupper(x)}'
```

Summary

I hope that you have a better and clearer understanding of what you can use the AWK tool for. This is a data-processing tool that runs through text files, line by line, and processes the code you add. The main block runs for each line that matches the row criteria, whereas the BEGIN and END block code is executed just once.

You've learned how to use AWK built-in variables and how to define your own variables and use them.

Also, you have learned how to use the if, while, and for loop to iterate over data fields.

In the next chapter, we will discuss regular expressions and how to use them in sed and AWK to gain a lot of power.

Questions

1. What is the output of the following command?

```
$ awk '
BEGIN{
var="I love AWK tool"
print $var
}'
```

2. Assume you have the following file:

```
13
15
22
18
35
27
```

Then you run the following command against this file:

```
$ awk '{if ($1 > 30) print $2}' myfile
```

How many numbers will be printed?

3. Assume that you have the following file:

```
135 325 142
215 325 152
147 254 327
```

And you run the following command:

```
$ awk '{
total = 0
i = 1
while (i < 3)
{
total += $i
i++
}
mean = total / 3
print "Mean value:",mean
}' myfile
```

What is wrong with the previous code?

4. How many lines will be printed from the following command?

```
$ awk -F":" '$3 < 1 ' /etc/passwd
```

Further reading

Please see the following for further reading relating to this chapter:

- https://likegeeks.com/awk-command/
- https://www.gnu.org/software/gawk/manual/gawk.html

11
Regular Expressions

In this chapter, we will talk about the most mysterious part of using **stream editor** (**sed**) and AWK. They are regular expressions, or regexes for short. In the previous chapters, we discussed some regular expressions shyly and that's because we don't need to dig into them without a good understanding.

If you understand how regular expressions are written, you will save a lot of time and effort. With regular expressions, you will unleash the real power behind sed and AWK and will use them professionally.

This chapter will cover the following aspects:

- Regular expression engines
- Defining BRE patterns
- Defining ERE patterns
- Using `grep`

Technical requirements

The source code for this chapter can be downloaded here:

```
https://github.com/PacktPublishing/Mastering-Linux-Shell-Scripting-Second-
Edition/tree/master/Chapter11
```

Regular expression engines

To start with, what are regular expressions?

Regular expressions are strings that the regex engine interprets to match a specific text. It's like an advanced way of searching.

Assume that you want to search a file for lines starting with any small letters, or you want to search for lines that contain a number, or maybe search for lines starting with specific text. The normal search can't be generic: the only way to do that is to use regular expressions.

And what is the regex engine?

The regex engine is the piece of software that understands these strings and translates them to find the matched text.

There are many regex engines out there; for example, the engines that are shipped with programming languages such as Java, Perl, and Python. Also, the engines that Linux tools use are sed and AWK, and the important thing for us now is to learn the types of regex engine in Linux.

There are two types of regex engine in Linux:

- The **Basic Regular Expression (BRE)** engine
- The **Extended Regular Expression (ERE)** engine

Most Linux binaries understand both engines, such as sed and AWK.

`grep` also can understand ERE, but you have to use the `-E` option, which is equivalent to using `egrep`.

We will see how to define a regex pattern for sed and AWK. We will start by defining BRE patterns, so let's get started.

Defining BRE patterns

To define a regex pattern, you can type the following:

```
$ echo "Welcome to shell scripting" | sed -n '/shell/p'
$ echo "Welcome to shell scripting" | awk '/shell/{print $0}'
```

likegeeks@likegeeks-VirtualBox ~/Desktop

File Edit View Search Terminal Help

```
likegeeks@likegeeks-VirtualBox ~/Desktop $ echo "Welcome to shell scripting" | sed -n '/shell/p'
Welcome to shell scripting
likegeeks@likegeeks-VirtualBox ~/Desktop $ echo "Welcome to shell scripting" | awk '/shell/{print
$0}'
Welcome to shell scripting
likegeeks@likegeeks-VirtualBox ~/Desktop $ 
```

A very important thing you need to know about regex patterns in general is they are case sensitive:

```
$ echo "Welcome to shell scripting" | awk '/shell/{print $0}'
$ echo "Welcome to SHELL scripting" | awk '/shell/{print $0}'
```

likegeeks@likegeeks-VirtualBox ~/Desktop

File Edit View Search Terminal Help

```
likegeeks@likegeeks-VirtualBox ~/Desktop $ echo "Welcome to shell scripting" | awk '/shell/{print
$0}'
Welcome to shell scripting
likegeeks@likegeeks-VirtualBox ~/Desktop $ echo "Welcome to SHELL scripting" | awk '/shell/{print
$0}'
likegeeks@likegeeks-VirtualBox ~/Desktop $ 
```

Say you want to match any of the following characters:

```
.*[]^${}\+?|()
```

You must escape them with a backslash because these characters are special characters for the regex engines.

Now you know how to define a BRE pattern. Let's use the common BRE characters.

Anchor characters

Anchor characters are used to match the beginning or the end of a line. There are two anchor characters: the caret (^) and the dollar sign ($).

The caret character is used to match the beginning of a line:

```
$ echo "Welcome to shell scripting" | awk '/^Welcome/{print $0}'
$ echo "SHELL scripting" | awk '/^Welcome/{print $0}'
$ echo "Welcome to shell scripting" | sed -n '/^Welcome/p'
```

So, the caret character is used to check whether the specified text is at the beginning of the line.

If you want to search for the caret as a character, you should escape it with a backslash if you use AWK.

However, if you use sed, you don't need to escape it:

```
$ echo "Welcome ^ is a test" | awk '/\^/{print $0}'
$ echo "Welcome ^ to shell scripting" | sed -n '/^/p'
```

To match the end of the text, you can use the dollar sign character ($):

```
$ echo "Welcome to shell scripting" | awk '/scripting$/{print $0}'
$ echo "Welcome to shell scripting" | sed -n '/scripting$/p'
```

```
                          likegeeks@likegeeks-VirtualBox ~/Desktop                    —  +  x
 File  Edit  View  Search  Terminal  Help
likegeeks@likegeeks-VirtualBox ~/Desktop $ echo "Welcome to shell scripting" | awk '/scripting$/{print $0}'
Welcome to shell scripting
likegeeks@likegeeks-VirtualBox ~/Desktop $ echo "Welcome to shell scripting" | sed -n '/scripting$/p'
Welcome to shell scripting
likegeeks@likegeeks-VirtualBox ~/Desktop $ ▮
```

You can use both characters (^) and ($) in the same pattern to specify text.

You can use these characters to do something useful, such as search for empty lines and trim them:

```
$ awk '!/^$/{print $0}' myfile
```

The exclamation mark (!) is called the negation character, which negates what's after it.

The pattern searches for ^$ where the caret (^) refers to the beginning of a line and the dollar sign ($) refers to the end of a line, which means search for lines that have nothing between the beginning and the end which means empty lines. Then we negate that with the exclamation mark (!) to get the other lines that are not empty.

Let's apply it to the following file:

```
Lorem Ipsum is simply dummy text .
Lorem Ipsum has been the industry's standard dummy.
It has survived not only five centuries
It is a long established fact that a reader will be distracted.
```

Now, let's see the magic:

```
$ awk '!/^$/{print $0}' myfile
```

```
                          likegeeks@likegeeks-VirtualBox ~/Desktop                    —  +  x
 File  Edit  View  Search  Terminal  Help
likegeeks@likegeeks-VirtualBox ~/Desktop $ awk '!/^$/{print $0}' myfile
Lorem Ipsum is simply dummy text .
Lorem Ipsum has been the industry's standard dummy.
It has survived not only five centuries
It is a long established fact that a reader will be distracted.
likegeeks@likegeeks-VirtualBox ~/Desktop $ ▮
```

The lines are printed without the empty lines.

The dot character

The dot character matches any character except the new line (\n). Let's use it against the following file:

```
Welcome to shell scripting.
I love shell scripting.
shell scripting is awesome.
```

Say we use the following commands:

```
$ awk '/.sh/{print $0}' myfile
$ sed -n '/.sh/p' myfile
```

This pattern matches any line containing sh and any text before it:

As you can see, it matches the first two lines only because the third line starts with sh, so no match for the third line.

The character class

We saw how to match any character using the dot character. What if you want to match a specific set of characters only?

You can pass the characters you want to match between square brackets [] to match them, and this is the character class.

Let's take the following file as an example:

```
I love bash scripting.
I hope it works without a crash.
Or I'll smash it.
```

Let's see how the character class works:

```
$ awk '/[mbr]ash/{print $0}' myfile
$ sed -n '/[mbr]ash/p' myfile
```

The character class `[mbr]` matches any of the included characters followed by ash, so this matches the three lines.

You can employ it in something useful, such as matching an uppercase or a lower case character:

```
$ echo "Welcome to shell scripting" | awk '/^[Ww]elcome/{print $0}'
$ echo "welcome to shell scripting" | awk '/^[Ww]elcome/{print $0}'
```

The character class is negated using the caret character like this:

```
$ awk '/[^br]ash/{print $0}' myfile
```

Here, we match any line that contains ash and starts neither with b nor r.

> Remember that using the caret character (^) outside the square brackets means the beginning of a line.

Using character class, you specify your characters. What if you have a long range of characters?

Ranges of characters

You can specify a range of characters to match between square brackets as follows:

```
[a-d]
```

This means the range of characters from a to d, so a, b, c, and d are included.

Let's use the same previous example file:

```
$ awk '/[a-m]ash/{print $0}' myfile
$ sed -n '/[a-m]ash/p' myfile
```

The character range from a to m is selected. The third line contains r before ash, which is not in our range, so only the second line doesn't match.

You can use numbers ranges as well:

```
$ awk '/[0-9]/'
```

This pattern means from 0 to 9 is matched.

You can write multiple ranges in the same bracket:

```
$ awk '/[d-hm-z]ash/{print $0}' myfile
$ sed -n '/[d-hm-z]ash/p' myfile
```

In this pattern, from d to h and from m to z are selected and since the first line contains b before ash, only the first line doesn't match.

You can use the ranges to select all uppercase and lowercase characters as follows:

```
$ awk '/[a-zA-Z]/'
```

Special character classes

We saw how to match a set of characters using the character class, then we saw how to match a range of characters using character ranges.

Actually, the ERE engine offers ready-to-use classes to match some common sets of characters as follows:

[[:alpha:]]	Matches any alphabetical character
[[:upper:]]	Matches A–Z uppercase only
[[:lower:]]	Matches a–z lowercase only
[[:alnum:]]	Matches 0–9, A–Z, or a–z
[[:blank:]]	Matches space or Tab only
[[:space:]]	Matches any whitespace character: space, Tab, CR
[[:digit:]]	Matches from 0 to 9
[[:print:]]	Matches any printable character
[[:punct:]]	Matches any punctuation character

So, if you want to match uppercase characters, you can use [[:upper:]] and it will work exactly as the character range [A-Z].

Let's test one of them against the following example file:

```
checking special character classes.
This LINE contains upper case.
ALSO this one.
```

We will match the uppercase characters to see how it works:

```
$ awk '/[[:upper:]]/{print $0}' myfile
$ sed -n '/[[:upper:]]/p' myfile
```

The uppercase special class makes it easy to match any line that contains uppercase letters.

The asterisk

The asterisk is used to match the existence of a character or a character class zero or more times.

This can be useful when searching for a word with multiple variations or that has been misspelled:

```
$ echo "Checking colors" | awk '/colou*rs/{print $0}'
$ echo "Checking colours" | awk '/colou*rs/{print $0}'
```

If the character u doesn't exist at all or exists, that will match the pattern.

We can benefit from the asterisk character by using it with the dot character to match any number of characters.

Let's see how to use them against the following example file:

```
This is a sample line
And this is another one
This is one more
Finally, the last line is this
```

Let's write a pattern that matches any line that contains the word `this` and anything after it:

```
$ awk '/this.*/{print $0}' myfile
$ sed -n '/ this.*/p' myfile
```

```
                      likegeeks@likegeeks-VirtualBox ~/Desktop              —  +  ×
 File  Edit  View  Search  Terminal  Help
likegeeks@likegeeks-VirtualBox ~/Desktop $ awk '/this.*/{print $0}' myfile
And this is another one
Finally, the last line is this
likegeeks@likegeeks-VirtualBox ~/Desktop $ sed -n '/ this.*/p' myfile
And this is another one
Finally, the last line is this
likegeeks@likegeeks-VirtualBox ~/Desktop $ █
```

The fourth line contains the word `this`, but the first and third lines contain a capital `T`, so that it doesn't match.

The second line contains the word and text after it, whereas the fourth line contains the word and nothing after it, and in both cases, the asterisk matches zero or more instances.

You can use the asterisk with the character class to match the existence of any character inside the character class for one time or none at all.

```
$ echo "toot" | awk '/t[aeor]*t/{print $0}'
$ echo "tent" | awk '/t[aeor]*t/{print $0}'
$ echo "tart" | awk '/t[aeor]*t/{print $0}'
```

```
                      likegeeks@likegeeks-VirtualBox ~/Desktop              —  +  ×
 File  Edit  View  Search  Terminal  Help
likegeeks@likegeeks-VirtualBox ~/Desktop $ echo "toot" | awk '/t[aeor]*t/{print $0}'
toot
likegeeks@likegeeks-VirtualBox ~/Desktop $ echo "tent" | awk '/t[aeor]*t/{print $0}'
likegeeks@likegeeks-VirtualBox ~/Desktop $ echo "tart" | awk '/t[aeor]*t/{print $0}'
tart
likegeeks@likegeeks-VirtualBox ~/Desktop $ █
```

The first line contains the character o two times, so it matches.

The second line contains the n character, which doesn't exist in the character class, so there is no match.

The third line contains the characters a and r, once for each, and they exist in the character class, so that line matches the pattern too.

Defining ERE patterns

We saw how easy it is to define BRE patterns. Now, we will see some ERE patterns, which are more powerful.

ERE engines understand the following patterns besides BRE patterns:

- Question marks
- Plus signs
- Curly braces
- Pipe characters
- Expression grouping

By default, AWK supports ERE patterns, and sed needs -r to understand these patterns.

The question mark

The question mark matches the existence of the preceding character or character class zero or one time only:

```
$ echo "tt" | awk '/to?t/{print $0}'
$ echo "tot" | awk '/to?t/{print $0}'
$ echo "toot" | awk '/to?t/{print $0}'
$ echo "tt" | sed -r -n '/to?t/p'
$ echo "tot" | sed -r -n '/to?t/p'
$ echo "toot" | sed -r -n '/to?t/p'
```

```
                    likegeeks@likegeeks-VirtualBox ~/Desktop            —  +  ×
 File  Edit  View  Search  Terminal  Help
likegeeks@likegeeks-VirtualBox ~/Desktop $ echo "tt" | awk '/to?t/{print $0}'
tt
likegeeks@likegeeks-VirtualBox ~/Desktop $ echo "tot" | awk '/to?t/{print $0}'
tot
likegeeks@likegeeks-VirtualBox ~/Desktop $ echo "toot" | awk '/to?t/{print $0}'
likegeeks@likegeeks-VirtualBox ~/Desktop $ echo "tt" | sed -r -n '/to?t/p'
tt
likegeeks@likegeeks-VirtualBox ~/Desktop $ echo "tot" | sed -r -n '/to?t/p'
tot
likegeeks@likegeeks-VirtualBox ~/Desktop $ echo "toot" | sed -r -n '/to?t/p'
likegeeks@likegeeks-VirtualBox ~/Desktop $ █
```

In the first two examples, the character o exists zero and one time, whereas in the third example, it exists two times, which doesn't match the pattern

In the same way, you can use the question mark with the character class:

```
$ echo "tt" | awk '/t[oa]?t/{print $0}'
$ echo "tot" | awk '/t[oa]?t/{print $0}'
$ echo "toot" | awk '/t[oa]?t/{print $0}'
$ echo "tt" | sed -r -n '/t[oa]?t/p'
$ echo "tot" | sed -r -n '/t[oa]?t/p'
$ echo "toot" | sed -r -n '/t[oa]?t/p'
```

```
                    likegeeks@likegeeks-VirtualBox ~/Desktop            —  +  ×
 File  Edit  View  Search  Terminal  Help
likegeeks@likegeeks-VirtualBox ~/Desktop $ echo "tt" | awk '/t[oa]?t/{print $0}'
tt
likegeeks@likegeeks-VirtualBox ~/Desktop $ echo "tot" | awk '/t[oa]?t/{print $0}'
tot
likegeeks@likegeeks-VirtualBox ~/Desktop $ echo "toot" | awk '/t[oa]?t/{print $0}'
likegeeks@likegeeks-VirtualBox ~/Desktop $ echo "tt" | sed -r -n '/t[oa]?t/p'
tt
likegeeks@likegeeks-VirtualBox ~/Desktop $ echo "tot" | sed -r -n '/t[oa]?t/p'
tot
likegeeks@likegeeks-VirtualBox ~/Desktop $ echo "toot" | sed -r -n '/t[oa]?t/p'
likegeeks@likegeeks-VirtualBox ~/Desktop $ █
```

The third example only doesn't match because it contains the o character two times.

Note that when using the question mark with the character class, it doesn't need to have all of character class in the text; one is enough to pass the pattern

The plus sign

The plus sign matches the existence of the preceding character or character class one time or more, so it must exist at least once:

```
$ echo "tt" | awk '/to+t/{print $0}'
$ echo "tot" | awk '/to+t/{print $0}'
$ echo "toot" | awk '/to+t/{print $0}'
$ echo "tt" | sed -r -n '/to+t/p'
$ echo "tot" | sed -r -n '/to+t/p'
$ echo "toot" | sed -r -n '/to+t/p'
```

```
                    likegeeks@likegeeks-VirtualBox ~/Desktop          - + ×
File  Edit  View  Search  Terminal  Help
likegeeks@likegeeks-VirtualBox ~/Desktop $ echo "tt"   | awk '/to+t/{print $0}'
likegeeks@likegeeks-VirtualBox ~/Desktop $ echo "tot"  | awk '/to+t/{print $0}'
tot
likegeeks@likegeeks-VirtualBox ~/Desktop $ echo "toot" | awk '/to+t/{print $0}'
toot
likegeeks@likegeeks-VirtualBox ~/Desktop $ echo "tt"   | sed -r -n '/to+t/p'
likegeeks@likegeeks-VirtualBox ~/Desktop $ echo "tot"  | sed -r -n '/to+t/p'
tot
likegeeks@likegeeks-VirtualBox ~/Desktop $ echo "toot" | sed -r -n '/to+t/p'
toot
likegeeks@likegeeks-VirtualBox ~/Desktop $
```

The first example doesn't have an o character, and that's why it's the only example that has no match.

Also, we can use the plus sign with the character class:

```
$ echo "tt" | awk '/t[oa]+t/{print $0}'
$ echo "tot" | awk '/t[oa]+t/{print $0}'
$ echo "toot" | awk '/t[oa]+t/{print $0}
$ echo "tt" | sed -r -n '/t[oa]+t/p'
$ echo "tot" | sed -r -n '/t[oa]+t/p'
$ echo "toot" | sed -r -n '/t[oa]+t/p'
```

The first example only doesn't match because it contains no o character at all.

Curly braces

The curly braces define the number of existence of the preceding character or character class:

```
$ echo "tt"   | awk '/to{1}t/{print $0}'
$ echo "tot"  | awk '/to{1}t/{print $0}'
$ echo "toot" | awk '/to{1}t/{print $0}'
$ echo "tt"   | sed -r -n '/to{1}t/p'
$ echo "tot"  | sed -r -n '/to{1}t/p'
$ echo "toot" | sed -r -n '/to{1}t/p'
```

The third example doesn't contain any matches because the o character exists two times. So, what if you want to specify a more flexible number?

You can specify a range inside the curly braces:

```
$ echo "toot" | awk '/to{1,2}t/{print $0}'
$ echo "toot" | sed -r -n '/to{1,2}t/p'
```

Here, we match the o character if it exists one or two times.

Also, you can use the curly braces with the character class:

```
$ echo "tt" | awk '/t[oa]{1}t/{print $0}'
$ echo "tot" | awk '/t[oa]{1}t/{print $0}'
$ echo "toot" | awk '/t[oa]{1}t/{print $0}'
$ echo "tt" | sed -r -n '/t[oa]{1}t/p'
$ echo "tot" | sed -r -n '/t[oa]{1}t/p'
$ echo "toot" | sed -r -n '/t[oa]{1}t/p'
```

As expected, if any of the characters [oa] exists for one time, the pattern will match.

The pipe character

The pipe character (|) tells the regex engine to match any of the passed strings. So, if one of them exists, that is enough for the pattern to match. It's like a logical OR between the passed strings:

```
$ echo "welcome to shell scripting" | awk '/Linux|bash|shell/{print $0}'
$ echo "welcome to bash scripting" | awk '/Linux|bash|shell/{print $0}'
$ echo "welcome to Linux scripting" | awk '/Linux|bash|shell/{print $0}'
$ echo "welcome to shell scripting" | sed -r -n '/Linux|bash|shell/p'
$ echo "welcome to bash scripting" | sed -r -n '/Linux|bash|shell/p'
$ echo "welcome to Linux scripting" | sed -r -n '/Linux|bash|shell/p'
```

```
likegeeks@likegeeks-VirtualBox ~/Desktop                              _ + x
File  Edit  View  Search  Terminal  Help
likegeeks@likegeeks-VirtualBox ~/Desktop $ echo "welcome to shell scripting" | awk '/Linux|bas
h|shell/{print $0}'
welcome to shell scripting
likegeeks@likegeeks-VirtualBox ~/Desktop $ echo "welcome to bash scripting" | awk '/Linux|bash
|shell/{print $0}'
welcome to bash scripting
likegeeks@likegeeks-VirtualBox ~/Desktop $ echo "welcome to Linux scripting" | awk '/Linux|bas
h|shell/{print $0}'
welcome to Linux scripting
likegeeks@likegeeks-VirtualBox ~/Desktop $ echo "welcome to shell scripting" | sed -r -n '/Lin
ux|bash|shell/p'
welcome to shell scripting
likegeeks@likegeeks-VirtualBox ~/Desktop $ echo "welcome to bash scripting" | sed -r -n '/Linu
x|bash|shell/p'
welcome to bash scripting
likegeeks@likegeeks-VirtualBox ~/Desktop $ echo "welcome to Linux scripting" | sed -r -n '/Lin
ux|bash|shell/p'
welcome to Linux scripting
likegeeks@likegeeks-VirtualBox ~/Desktop $ █
```

All the previous examples have a match, since any of the three words exists in each example.

There are no spaces between the pipes and the words.

Expression grouping

You can use parentheses () to group characters or words to make them one piece in the eyes of the regex engine:

```
$ echo "welcome to shell scripting" | awk '/(shell scripting)/{print $0}'
$ echo "welcome to bash scripting" | awk '/(shell scripting)/{print $0}'
$ echo "welcome to shell scripting" | sed -r -n '/(shell scripting)/p'
$ echo "welcome to bash scripting" | sed -r -n '/(shell scripting)/p'
```

Since the `shell scripting` string is grouped with parentheses, it will be treated as a single piece.

So, if the entire sentence doesn't exist, the pattern will fail.

You may have realized that you can achieve that without parentheses like this:

```
$ echo "welcome to shell scripting" | sed -r -n '/shell scripting/p'
```

So, what is the benefit of using parentheses or expression grouping? Check the following examples to know the difference.

You can use any of the ERE characters with the grouping parentheses:

```
$ echo "welcome to shell scripting" | awk '/(bash scripting)?/{print $0}'
$ echo "welcome to shell scripting" | awk '/(bash scripting)+/{print $0}'
$ echo "welcome to shell scripting" | sed -r -n '/(bash scripting)?/p'
$ echo "welcome to shell scripting" | sed -r -n '/(bash scripting)+/p'
```

```
                          likegeeks@likegeeks-VirtualBox ~/Desktop                    – + x
 File  Edit  View  Search  Terminal  Help
 likegeeks@likegeeks-VirtualBox ~/Desktop $ echo "welcome to shell scripting" | awk '/(bash scr
 ipting)?/{print $0}'
 welcome to shell scripting
 likegeeks@likegeeks-VirtualBox ~/Desktop $ echo "welcome to shell scripting" | awk '/(bash scr
 ipting)+/{print $0}'
 likegeeks@likegeeks-VirtualBox ~/Desktop $ echo "welcome to shell scripting" | sed -r -n '/(ba
 sh scripting)?/p'
 welcome to shell scripting
 likegeeks@likegeeks-VirtualBox ~/Desktop $ echo "welcome to shell scripting" | sed -r -n '/(ba
 sh scripting)+/p'
 likegeeks@likegeeks-VirtualBox ~/Desktop $ █
```

In the first example, we search for the whole sentence `bash scripting` for zero or one time using the question mark, and because the whole sentence doesn't exist, the pattern succeeds.

Without expression grouping, you won't get the same result.

Using grep

If we wanted to talk properly about `grep`, an entire book would not be enough. `grep` supports many engines along with BRE and ERE. It supports engines such as **Perl-compatible regular expression (PCRE)**.

The `grep` is a very powerful tool that most system administrators use every day. We just want to enlighten the point of using BRE and ERE patterns as we did with sed and AWK.

`grep` tool understands BRE patterns by default, and if you want to use ERE patterns, you should use the `-E` option.

Let's work with the following example file and use a BRE pattern:

```
Welcome to shell scripting.
love shell scripting.
shell scripting is awesome.
```

Let's test a BRE pattern:

```
$ grep '.sh' myfile
```

```
                    likegeeks@likegeeks-VirtualBox ~/Desktop        _  +  x
 File  Edit  View  Search  Terminal  Help
likegeeks@likegeeks-VirtualBox ~/Desktop $ grep '.sh' myfile
Welcome to shell scripting.
I love shell scripting.
likegeeks@likegeeks-VirtualBox ~/Desktop $
```

The results are colored in red.

Let's test an ERE pattern:

```
$ grep -E 'to+' myfile
```

```
                    likegeeks@likegeeks-VirtualBox ~/Desktop        _  +  x
 File  Edit  View  Search  Terminal  Help
likegeeks@likegeeks-VirtualBox ~/Desktop $ grep -E 'to+' myfile
Welcome to shell scripting.
likegeeks@likegeeks-VirtualBox ~/Desktop $
```

All other ERE characters can be used in the same way.

Summary

In this chapter, we covered regular expressions and the regex engines BRE and ERE. We learned how to define patterns for them.

We learned how to write these patterns for sed, AWK, and grep.

Also, we saw how the special character classes make it easy to match sets of characters.

We saw how to use the powerful ERE patterns and how to group expressions.

Finally, we saw how to use the grep tool and how to define BRE and ERE patterns.

In the next two chapters, we will see some practical examples for AWK.

Questions

1. Assume that you have the following file:

    ```
    Welcome to shell scripting.
    I love shell scripting.
    shell scripting is awesome.
    ```

    Say you run the following command:

    ```
    $ awk '/awesome$/{print $0}' myfile
    ```

    How many lines will be printed in the output?

2. How many lines will be printed if we use the following command against the previous file?

    ```
    $ awk '/scripting\..*/{print $0}' myfile
    ```

3. How many lines will be printed if we use the following command against the previous sample file?

    ```
    $ awk '/^[Ww]?/{print $0}' myfile
    ```

4. What is the output of the following command?

    ```
    $ echo "welcome to shell scripting" | sed -n '/Linux|bash|shell/p'
    ```

Further reading

Please see the following for further reading related to this chapter:

*   https://www.regular-expressions.info/engine.html
*   http://tldp.org/LDP/Bash-Beginners-Guide/html/chap_04.html

12
Summarizing Logs with AWK

In the previous chapter, we talked about regular expressions and we saw how to use them to empower `sed` and AWK. In this chapter, we will discuss some practical examples of using AWK.

One of the tasks that AWK is really good at is filtering data from log files. These log files may be many lines in length, perhaps 250,000 or more. I have worked with data with over a million lines. AWK can process these lines quickly and effectively. As an example, we will work with a web server access log with 30,000 lines to show how effective and well-written AWK code can be. As we work our way through the chapter, we will also see different log files and review some of the techniques that we can employ with the `awk` command and the AWK programming language to help with the reporting and administration of our services. In this chapter, we will cover the following topics:

- HTTPD log file format
- Displaying data from web logs
- Displaying the highest ranking client IP addresses
- Displaying the browser data
- Working with email logs

Technical requirements

The source code for this chapter can be downloaded from here:

```
https://github.com/PacktPublishing/Mastering-Linux-Shell-Scripting-Second-
Edition/tree/master/Chapter12
```

The HTTPD log file format

When working with any file, the first task is to become familiar with the file schema. In simple terms, we need to know what is represented by each field and what is used to delimit the fields. We will be working with the access log file from an Apache HTTPD web server. The location of the log file can be controlled from the `httpd.conf` file. The default log file location on a Debian-based system is `/var/log/apache2/access.log`; other systems may use the `httpd` directory in place of `apache2`.

The `log` file is already in the code bundle, so you can download it and use it directly.

Using the `tail` command, we can display the end of the `log` file. Although, to be fair, the use of `cat` will do just as well with this file, as it will have just a few lines:

```
$ tail /var/log/apache2/access.log
```

The output of the command and the contents of the file are shown in the following screenshot:

```
root@andrew-15-10:~# tail /var/log/apache2/access.log
127.0.0.1 - - [12/Oct/2015:09:48:42 +0100] "GET / HTTP/1.1" 200 3525 "-" "Mozilla/5.0 (X11; Ubuntu; L
inux x86_64; rv:41.0) Gecko/20100101 Firefox/41.0"
127.0.0.1 - - [12/Oct/2015:09:48:43 +0100] "GET /icons/ubuntu-logo.png HTTP/1.1" 200 3689 "http://loc
alhost/" "Mozilla/5.0 (X11; Ubuntu; Linux x86_64; rv:41.0) Gecko/20100101 Firefox/41.0"
127.0.0.1 - - [12/Oct/2015:09:48:43 +0100] "GET /favicon.ico HTTP/1.1" 404 500 "-" "Mozilla/5.0 (X11;
 Ubuntu; Linux x86_64; rv:41.0) Gecko/20100101 Firefox/41.0"
127.0.0.1 - - [12/Oct/2015:09:48:43 +0100] "GET /favicon.ico HTTP/1.1" 404 500 "-" "Mozilla/5.0 (X11;
 Ubuntu; Linux x86_64; rv:41.0) Gecko/20100101 Firefox/41.0"
```

The output does wrap a little onto the new lines, but we do get a feel of the layout of the log. We can also see that even though we feel that we access just one web page, we are in fact accessing two items: the `index.html` and the `ubuntu-logo.png`. We also failed to access the `favicon.ico` file. We can see that the file is space separated. The meaning of each of the fields is laid out in the following table:

Field	Purpose
1	Client IP address.
2	Client identity as defined by RFC 1413 and the `identd` client. This is not read unless `IdentityCheck` is enabled. If it is not read, the value will be with a hyphen.
3	The user ID of the user authentication if enabled. If authentication is not enabled, the value will be a hyphen.

4	The date and time of the request in the format of `day/month/year:hour:minute:second offset`.
5	The actual request and method.
6	The return status code, such as `200` or `404`.
7	File size in bytes.

Even though these fields are defined by Apache, we have to be careful. The time, date, and time zone is a single field and is defined within square braces; however, there are additional spaces inside the field between that data and the time zone. To ensure that we print the complete time field if required, we need to print both $4 and $5. This is shown in the following command example:

```
$ awk ' { print $4,$5 } ' /var/log/apache2/access.log
```

We can view the command and the output it produces in the following screenshot:

```
root@andrew-15-10:~# awk ' { print $4, $5 } ' /var/log/apache2/access.log
[12/Oct/2015:09:48:42 +0100]
[12/Oct/2015:09:48:43 +0100]
[12/Oct/2015:09:48:43 +0100]
[12/Oct/2015:09:48:43 +0100]
```

Displaying data from web logs

We have already had a preview of how we can use AWK to view the log files from the Apache web server; however, we will now move onto our demonstration file that has greater and more varied content.

Selecting entries by date

Having seen how we can display the date, we should perhaps look at how we print entries from just one day. To do this, we can use the match operator in `awk`. This is denoted by the tilde or squiggly line, if you prefer. As we only need the date element, there is no need for us to use both the date and time zone field. The following command shows how to print entries from September 10, 2014:

```
$ awk ' ( $4 ~ /10\/Sep\/2014/ ) ' access.log
```

For completeness, this command and partial output is shown in the following screenshot:

```
pi@pilabs ~/bin $ awk '( $4 ~ /10\/Sep\/2014/ )' access.log  | less
128.252.139.84 - - [10/Sep/2014:00:00:03 +0100] "GET /wp/?cat=281 HTTP/1.1" 200
51860 "http://theurbanpenguin.com/wp/?cat=281" "Mozilla/5.0 (Macintosh; Intel M
c OS X 10_8_5) AppleWebKit/537.36 (KHTML, like Gecko) Chrome/36.0.1985.125 Safa
i/537.36"
41.150.168.184 - - [10/Sep/2014:00:00:23 +0100] "GET /scripting/java.html HTTP/
```

The round brackets or parentheses embrace the range of lines that we are looking for and we have omitted the main block, which ensures that we print the complete matching lines from the range. There is nothing stopping us from further filtering on the fields to print from the matching lines. For example, if we want to print out just the client IP address that is being used to access the web server, we can print field 1. This is shown in the following command example:

```
$ awk ' ( $4 ~ /10\/Sep\/2014/ ) { print $1 } ' access.log
```

If we want to be able to print the total number of accesses on a given date, we could pipe the entries through to the wc command. This is demonstrated in the following:

```
$ awk ' ( $4 ~ /10\/Sep\/2014/ ) { print $1 } ' access.log | wc -l
```

However, if we want to use awk to do this for us, this will be more efficient than starting a new process and we can count the entries. If we use the built-in variable NR, we can print entire lines in the files, not just those within the range. It is best to increment our own variable in the main block instead of matching the range for each line. The END block can be implemented to print the count variable we use. The following command line acts as an example:

```
$ awk ' ( $4 ~ /10\/Sep\/2014/ ) { print $1; COUNT++ }  END { print COUNT
}' access.log
```

The output of the count from both wc and the internal counter will give us 16205 as a result from the demonstration file. We should use the variable increment within the main block if we want to count and nothing else:

```
$ awk ' ( $4 ~ /10\/Sep\/2014/ ) { COUNT++ }  END { print COUNT }'
access.log
```

We can see this in the following output:

```
pi@pilabs ~/bin $ awk '( $4 ~ /10\/Sep\/2014/ ) { COUNT++ } END { print COUNT } ' access.log
16205
pi@pilabs ~/bin $ _
```

Summarizing 404 errors

The status code of the request page is shown in field 9 of the log. The 404 status will represent the page not found error on the server. I am sure we have all seen that in our browsers at some stage. This may be indicative of a misconfigured link on your site or just produced by a browser searching for the icon image to display in tabbed browsers for the page. You can also identify potential threats to your site by requests looking for standard pages that may give access to additional information on PHP driven sites, such as WordPress.

Firstly, we can solely print the status of the request:

```
$ awk '{ print $9 } ' access.log
```

We can now extend the code a little as well as ourselves and just print the 404 errors:

```
$ awk ' ( $9 ~ /404/ ) { print $9 } ' access.log
```

We can extend this a little further by printing both the status code and the page that was being accessed. This will need us to print field 9 and field 7. Simply put, this will be as shown in the following code:

```
$ awk ' ( $9 ~ /404/ ) { print $9, $7 } ' access.log
```

Many of these failed accessed pages will be duplicated. To summarize these records, we can use the command pipeline to achieve this with the sort and uniq commands:

```
$ awk ' ( $9 ~ /404/ ) { print $9, $7 } ' access.log | sort -u
```

To use the uniq command, the data must be pre-sorted; hence, we use the sort command to prepare the data.

Summarizing HTTP access codes

It is time for us to leave the pure command line and start working with the AWK control files. As always, when the complexity of the required result set increases, we see an increase in the complexity of the awk code. We will create a status.awk file in our current directory. The file should look similar to the following file:

```
{ record[$9]++ }
END {
for (r in record)
print r, " has occurred ", record[r], " times." }
```

First, we will strip down the main code block and this is very simple and sparse. This is a simple way to count each unique occurrence of a status code. Instead of using a simple variable, we feed this into an array. The array in this case is called a record. An array is a multi-values variable and the slots in the array are known as keys. So we will have a collection of variables stored in the array. For example, we expect to see entries for record[200] and record[404]. We populate each key with their occurrence count. Each time we find a 404 code, we increment the count that is stored in the associated key:

```
{ record[$9]++ }
```

In the END block, we create the summary information using a for loop to print out each key and value from the array:

```
END {
for (r in record)
print r, " has occurred ", record[r], " times." }
```

To run this, the associated command line will be similar to the following:

```
$ awk -f status.awk access.log
```

To view the command and output, we have included the following screenshot:

```
pi@pilabs ~/bin $ awk -f status.awk access.log
200  has occurred  23825  times.
206  has occurred  48  times.
301  has occurred  60  times.
302  has occurred  21  times.
304  has occurred  2273  times.
403  has occurred  133  times.
404  has occurred  4382  times.
501  has occurred  63  times.
pi@pilabs ~/bin $ _
```

We can take this further and focus on the 404 errors. You could, of course, choose any of the status codes. We can see from the results that we have 4382 404 status codes. To summarize these 404 codes, we will copy the status.awk to a new file named 404.awk. We can edit the 404.awk adding an if statement to work only on the 404 codes. The file should be similar to the following code:

```
{ if ( $9 == "404" )
    record[$9,$7]++ }
END {
for (r in record)
print r, " has occurred ", record[r], " times." }
```

If we execute the code with the following command:

```
$ awk -f 404.awk access.log
```

The output will be similar to the following screenshot:

```
pi@pilabs ~/bin $ awk -f 404.awk access.log
404/old/wp-admin/  has occurred  2  times.
404/monitor.html  has occurred  1  times.
404/windows.html  has occurred  1  times.
404/novell.html  has occurred  1  times.
404/user/  has occurred  2  times.
404/linux.html  has occurred  1  times.
404/zcm10.html  has occurred  1  times.
```

Resources hits

You can check how many times a specific page or a resource was requested using AWK:

```
$ awk '{print $7}' access.log | sort | uniq -c | sort -rn
```

The preceding command will sort the requested resources from the highest requested resource to the lowest:

```
                    likegeeks@likegeeks-VirtualBox ~/Desktop        _  +  ×
File  Edit  View  Search  Terminal  Help
   3468 /favicon.ico
   2330 /wp/wp-content/themes/twentytwelve/style.css?ver=3.9.1
   2265 /wp/wp-content/themes/twentytwelve/js/navigation.js?ver=20140711
   2199 /wp/wp-includes/js/jquery/jquery.js?ver=1.11.0
   2187 /wp/wp-includes/js/jquery/jquery-migrate.min.js?ver=1.2.1
   2024 /wp/wp-content/uploads/2014/05/cropped-wp3.png
    709 /wp/?feed=rss2
    507 /
    334 /wp/?p=2407
    329 /stylesheets/screen.css
    328 /stylesheets/style.css
    323 /wp/?p=2415
    302 /stylesheets/Softplain.ttf
    293 /images/favicon.ico
    286 /wp/wp-content/uploads/2013/11/raspi-config1-300x96.png
    284 /wp/wp-content/uploads/2013/11/tailshadow.png
    256 /wp/wp-content/uploads/2013/11/pdbedit.png
    255 /wp/wp-content/uploads/2013/11/shares-300x123.png
    255 /wp/wp-content/uploads/2013/11/backup.png
    248 /images/tup-coloured1.png
    243 /stylesheets/newstyle.css
```

The resources could be images, text files, or CSS files.

If you want to look at the requested PHP files, you can use `grep` to get PHP files only:

```
$ awk ' ($7 ~ /php/) {print $7}' access.log | sort | uniq -c | sort -nr
```

```
likegeeks@likegeeks-VirtualBox ~/Desktop          - + x
File  Edit  View  Search  Terminal  Help
    74 /wp/xmlrpc.php
    62 /wp/?p=1529/wp-login.php
    58 /wp/xmlrpc.php?rsd
    21 /wp/wp-login.php
    19 /wp/wp-login.php?registration=disabled
    19 /wp/wp-login.php?action=register
     6 /wp-login.php
     5 /admin.php
     4 /administrator/index.php
     3 /wp/wp-trackback.php?p=3043
     3 /wp/wp-trackback.php?p=1048
     3 /wp/wp-content/uploads/2013/08/php.png
     2 /wp/wp-trackback.php?p=586
     2 /wp/wp-trackback.php?p=3149
     2 /wp/wp-trackback.php?p=3085
     2 /lamp/php.html
     2 /bitrix/admin/index.php?lang=en
     2 /admin/login.php
     1 /xmlrpc.php
     1 /wp/wp-trackback.php?p=830
     1 /wp/wp-trackback.php?p=2357
     1 /wp/wp-trackback.php?p=2105
     1 /wp/wp-trackback.php?p=1805
     1 /wp//wp-content/uploads/wysija/themes/clefault/index.php
```

Alongside each page, there is the number of hits.

You can grab any statistics from the `log` file and get unique values and sort them the same way.

Identify image hotlinking

As we talk about resources, there is a problem that you may face, which is image hotlinking. It's about using your images from other servers by linking to them. This behavior of image hotlinking can leak your bandwidth.

And since we are talking about AWK, we will see how to use AWK to find out how it is using our images:

```
$ awk -F\" '($2 ~ /\.(png|jpg|gif)/ && $4 !~
/^https:\/\/www\.yourdomain\.com/){print $4}' access.log | sort | uniq -c |
sort
```

Note that you can prevent image hotlinking by a small `.htaccess` file if you are using Apache, by checking if the referrer is not your domain:

```
RewriteEngine on
RewriteCond %{HTTP_REFERER} !^$
RewriteCond %{HTTP_REFERER} !^https://(www\.)yourdomain.com/.*$ [NC]
RewriteRule \.(gif|jpg|jpeg|bmp|png)$ - [F]
```

Displaying the highest ranking IP address

You should now be aware of some the powers of `awk` and how immense the language structure is in itself. The data we have been able to produce from the 30,000 line file is truly powerful and easily extracted. We just need to replace the field we have used before with `$1`. This field represents the client IP address. If we make use of the following code, we will be able to print each IP Address and also the number of times it has been used to access the web server:

```
{ ip[$1]++ }
END {
for (i in ip)
print i, " has accessed the server ", ip[i], " times." }
```

We want to be able to extend this to show only the highest ranking IP address, the address that has been used the most to access the site. The work, again, will mainly be in the END block and will make use of a comparison against the current highest ranking address. The following file can be created and saved as `ip.awk`:

```
{ ip[$1]++ }
END {
for (i in ip)
    if ( max < ip[i] ) {
        max = ip[i]
        maxnumber = i }

print i, " has accessed ", ip[i], " times." }
```

We can see the output of the command in the following screenshot. Part of the client IP address has been obscured as it is from my public web server:

```
pi@pilabs ~/bin $
pi@pilabs ~/bin $ awk -f ip.awk access.log
121.   .52.100  has accessed  12  times.
pi@pilabs ~/bin $ _
```

The functionality of the code comes from within the END block. On entering the END block, we run into a for loop. We iterate through each entry in the ip array. We use the conditional if statement to see whether the current value that we are iterating through is higher than the current maximum. If it is, this becomes the new highest entry. When the loop has finished, we print the IP address that has the highest entry.

Displaying the browser data

The browser that is used to access the website is contained within the log file in field 12. It may be interesting to display the list of browsers used to access your site. The following code will assist you in displaying the list of accesses by the reported browser:

```
{ browser[$12]++ }
END {
    for ( b in browser )
        print b, " has accessed ", browser[b], " times."
}
```

You can see how we can create little plugins to awk with these files and adjust the field and array names to suit. The output is shown in the following screenshot:

```
pi@pilabs ~/bin $ awk -f browser.awk access.log
"DoCoMo/2.0  has accessed  7  times.
"com.apple.WebKit.WebContent/10600.1.15  has accessed  4  times.
"Xenu  has accessed  3  times.
"-"  has accessed  90  times.
"PHP/5.3.14"  has accessed  1  times.
"FeedBot"  has accessed  8  times.
"OpenOffice/4.1.0"  has accessed  91  times.
"facebookexternalhit/1.1  has accessed  11  times.
""Mozilla/5.0  has accessed  7  times.
"Feed  has accessed  48  times.
"msnbot-UDiscovery/2.0b  has accessed  9  times.
"Twitterbot/1.0"  has accessed  94  times.
"AdsBot-Google  has accessed  10  times.
"Python-urllib/1.17"  has accessed  1  times.
"HTTP_Request2/2.1.1  has accessed  4  times.
"Mozilla/4.0  has accessed  1713  times.
```

Interestingly, we see that Mozilla 4 and 5 make up the majority of the requesting client. We see that Mozilla 4 is listed here 1713 times. The Mozilla/5.0 entry here is malformed with an extra double quote. It appears later with 27,000 accesses.

Working with email logs

We have worked with logs from the Apache HTTP web server. The reality is that we can apply the same ideals and methodology to any log file. We will take a look at Postfix mail logs. The mail log holds all activity from the SMTP server and we can then see who has been sending emails to whom. The log file is usually located at /var/log/mail.log. I will access this on my Ubuntu 15.10 server that has a local email delivery. All this means is that the STMP server is listening only to the localhost interface of 127.0.0.1.

The log format will change a little depending on the type of message. For example, $7 will contain from logs on outbound messages, whereas inbound messages will contain to.

If we want to list all the inbound messages to the SMTP server, we can use the following command:

```
$ awk '  ( $7 ~ /^to/ ) ' /var/log/mail.log
```

As the string to is very short, we can add identification to it by ensuring that the field begins with to using the ^. The command and output is shown in the following screenshot:

```
root@andrew-15-10:~# awk '( $7 ~ /^to/ )' /var/log/mail.log
Oct 12 17:00:47 andrew-15-10 postfix/local[10109]: 80346680E8: to=<root@andrew-15-10>, relay=local, d
elay=0.14, delays=0.09/0.05/0/0.01, dsn=2.0.0, status=sent (delivered to mailbox)
root@andrew-15-10:~#
```

It will be easy to extend the to or from searches to also include usernames. We can see the format of the delivered or received mail. Working with the same template we used with the Apache logs, we can easily display the highest recipient or sender.

Summary

We now have some heavy ammunition behind our text processing and we can begin to understand just how powerful AWK can be. Working with real data is particularly useful in gauging the performance and accuracy of our searches. Having begun working with simple Apache entries on the newly installed Ubuntu 15.10 Apache web server, we soon migrated to the larger sample data from a live web server. With 30,000 lines, this file gives us some real meat to work with and in no time, we were able to produce credible reports. We closed up the return to the Ubuntu 15.10 server to analyze the Postfix SMTP logs. We can see that we can very much drag and drop the technology that we have previously used into the new log files.

Next up, we stick with AWK and look at how we can report on the `lastlog` data and on flat XML files.

Questions

1. Which field in the `access_log` file contains the IP address?
2. What is the command used to count the lines processed by AWK?
3. How do you get IP addresses of unique visitors from the Apache access log file?
4. How do you get the most visited PHP page from the Apache access log file?

Further reading

Please see the following for further reading relating to this chapter:

- `https://httpd.apache.org/docs/1.3/logs.html`

13
A Better lastlog with AWK

We have already seen, in Chapter 12, *Summarizing Logs with AWK*, how we can create complex reports from large amounts of data mined from purely text files. Similarly, we can create extensive reports using the output from standard command-line tools, such as the lastlog tool. In itself, lastlog can report the last login time for all users. Often, though, we may wish to filter the output from lastlog. Perhaps you need to exclude user accounts that have never been used to log in to the system. It may also be irrelevant to report on root, as the account may be predominately used for sudo only and not used to record regularly for standard logins.

In working through this chapter, we will work with lastlog and formatting XML data. As this is the last chapter in which we investigate AWK, we will configure record separators. We have already seen the use of field separators in AWK but we can change the default record separator from a newline to something more specific to our needs. More specifically, within this chapter we will cover:

- Using AWK ranges to exclude data
- Conditions based on the number of fields
- Manipulating the AWK record separator to report on XML data

Technical requirements

The source code for this chapter can be downloaded here:

https://github.com/PacktPublishing/Mastering-Linux-Shell-Scripting-Second-Edition/tree/master/Chapter13

Using AWK ranges to exclude data

So far in this book, we have predominately looked at including data with ranges either for sed or for awk. With both of these tools, we can negate the range so that we exclude the specified rows. For a perfect explanation, we will use the output from the lastlog command. This will print all the login data for all the users, including accounts that have never been logged in. These accounts that have never been logged in might be service accounts or for new users that have not logged into the system so far.

The lastlog command

If we look at the output from lastlog, when it is used without any options, we can begin to understand the issue. From the command line, we execute the command as a standard user. There is no requirement to run it as the root account. The command is shown in the following example:

```
$ lastlog
```

The partial output is shown within the following screenshot:

```
gdm                                        **Never logged in**
sshd                                       **Never logged in**
tcpdump                                    **Never logged in**
tux              pts/1     localhost       Tue Oct 20 13:02:35 +0100 2015
bob                                        **Never logged in**
u1                                         **Never logged in**
vboxadd                                    **Never logged in**
```

We can see, even from this limited output, that we have a cluttered output due to the virtual noise being created by the accounts that have not logged in. It is possible to alleviate this to some degree using the lastlog options but it may not entirely resolve the issue. To demonstrate this, we can add an option to lastlog to show standard users only and filter out other system and services users. This may vary on your system but on the sample CentOS 6 host that I am using, the first user will be UID 500. On CentOS 7, standard users UID starts from 1000.

If we use the lastlog -u 500-5000 command, we will only print data for those users with a UID within this range. On the simple demonstration system, we have just three user accounts for which the output is acceptable. However, we can understand that we may still have some clutter due to these accounts that have not yet been used. This is shown in the following screenshot:

```
centos6 ~ $ lastlog -u 500-5000
Username          Port    From          Latest
tux               pts/1   localhost     Tue Oct 20 13:02:35 +0100 2015
bob                                     **Never logged in**
u1                                      **Never logged in**
centos6 ~ $
```

In addition to the superfluous data being printed from Never logged in accounts, we may only be interested in the Username and Latest fields. This is another reason to support the need to use AWK as our data filter. In this way, we can provide both horizontal and vertical data filtering, rows, and columns.

Horizontally filtering rows with AWK

To provide this filtering using AWK, we will pipe the data from lastlog directly to awk. We will make use of a simple control file, initially providing the horizontal filtering or reducing the rows that we see. First, the command pipeline will be as simple as the following command example:

```
$ lastlog | awk -f lastlog.awk
```

Of course, the complexity is abstracted from the command line and concealed within the control file that we use. Initially, the control file is kept simple and reads as follows:

```
!(/Never logged in/ || /^Username/ || /^root/) {
  print $0;
}
```

The range is set up as we have seen previously and precedes the main code block. Using the exclamation mark in front of the parentheses negates or reverses the selected range. The double vertical bar acts as a logical OR. We do not include lines that contain Never logged in, nor do we include lines that start with Username. This removes the header-line that is printed by lastlog. Finally, we exclude the root account from the display. This initiates the rows that we work with and the main code block will print those lines.

Counting matched rows

We may also want to count the number of rows returned by the filter. For example, using the internal NR variable will show all rows and not just matched rows; for us to be able to report the number of users that have logged in, we must use our own variable. The following code will maintain the count within the variable that we name cnt. We increment this using the C style ++ for each iteration of the main code block.

We can use the END code block to display the closing value of this variable:

```
!(/Never logged in/ || /^Username/ || /^root/) {
  cnt++
  print $0;
}
END {
  print "========================="
  print "Total Number of Users Processed: ", cnt
}
```

We can see from the following code and output how this appears on my system:

```
centos6 ~ $ lastlog | awk -f ll.awk
tux             pts/1    localhost        Tue Oct 20 13:02:35 +0100 2015
=====================
Total Number of Users Processed:  1
centos6 ~ $ █
```

From the display output, we can now see that we show only users that have logged in and, in this case, it is just the single user. However, we may also decide that we want to abstract the data further and display only certain fields from the matched rows. This should be a simple task but it is complicated, as the number of fields will vary depending on how the login was executed.

Conditions based on the number of fields

If a user logs onto the server's physical console directly rather than logging on through a remote or graphical pseudo-terminal, then the lastlog output will not display the host field. To demonstrate this, I have logged on to my CentOS host directly to the tty1 console and avoided the GUI. The output from the previous AWK control file shows that we now have the users tux and bob; bob though lacks the host field as he is connected to a console:

```
centos6 ~ $ lastlog | awk -f ll.awk
tux             pts/1    192.168.0.3      Thu Oct 22 13:31:04 +0100 2015
bob             tty1                      Thu Oct 22 13:34:48 +0100 2015
=====================
Total Number of Users Processed:  2
centos6 ~ $ █
```

Although in itself it's not an issue, it will be if we want to filter the fields and the two row's field numbers will vary where a field is omitted from some lines. For `lastlog`, we will have 9 fields for most connections and only 8 fields for those that connect directly to the server console. The goal for the application is that we print the username and the date, but not the time of the last login. We will also print our own header in the BEGIN block. To ensure that we use the correct placements we will need to count the fields in each row using the NF internal variable.

For the 8 fields' lines we want to print fields 1, 4, 5, and 8; for the longer lines with additional host information, we will use fields 1, 5, 6 and 9. We will also use `printf` so that we can align the column data correctly. The control file should be edited, as shown in the following example:

```
BEGIN {
printf "%8s %11s\n","Username","Login date"
print "===================="
}
!(/Never logged in/ || /^Username/ || /^root/) {
cnt++
if ( NF == 8 )
    printf "%8s %2s %3s %4s\n", $1,$5,$4,$8

else
    printf "%8s %2s %3s %4s\n", $1,$6,$5,$9
}
END {
print "===================="
print "Total Number of Users Processed: ", cnt
}
```

We can see the command and the output it produces in the following screenshot. We can see how we can create a more suitable display based on information that we want to focus on:

```
centos6 ~ $ lastlog | awk -f ll.awk
Username  Login date
====================
     tux 22 Oct 2015
     bob 22 Oct 2015
====================
Total Number of Users Processed:  2
centos6 ~ $ ▮
```

If we look at the output, I have chosen to display the date before the month so we do not display the fields in numerical order. This, of course, is a personal choice and customizable to suit the way you feel the data should be displayed.

We can use the principles of what we have seen in the `lastlog` control file with output from any command and you should practice with the commands that you want to filter the data from.

Manipulating the AWK record separator to report on XML data

So far, while we have been working with AWK we have limited ourselves to working with individual rows, with each new row representing a new record. Although this is often what we want, where we work with tagged data, such as XML where an individual record may span multiple lines. In this case, we may need to look at setting the `RS` or `record` separator internal variable.

Apache Virtual Hosts

In Chapter 9, *Automating Apache Virtual Hosts*, we worked with **Apache Virtual Hosts**. This uses tagged data that defines the start and end of each virtual host. Even though we prefer to store each virtual host in its own file, they can be combined into a single file. Consider the following file that stores the possible virtual host definitions; this can be stored as the `virtualhost.conf` file, as shown:

```
<VirtualHost *:80>
DocumentRoot /www/example
ServerName www.example.org
# Other directives here
</VirtualHost>

<VirtualHost *:80>
DocumentRoot /www/theurbanpenguin
ServerName www.theurbanpenguin.com
# Other directives here
</VirtualHost>

<VirtualHost *:80>
DocumentRoot /www/packt
ServerName www.packtpub.com
```

```
# Other directives here
</VirtualHost>
```

We have the three virtual hosts within a single file. Each record is separated by an empty line, meaning that we have two new line characters that logically separate each entry. We will explain this to AWK by setting the RS variable as follows: RS="\n\n". With this in place, we can then print the required virtual host record. This will be set in the BEGIN code block of the control file.

We will also need to dynamically search the command line for the desired host configuration. We build this into the control file. The control file should look similar to the following code:

```
BEGIN { RS="\n\n" ; }
$0 ~ search { print }
```

The BEGIN block sets the variable and then we move onto the range. The range is set so that the record ($0) matches (~) the search variable. We must set the variable when awk is executed. The following command demonstrates the command line execution where the control file and configuration file are located within our working directory:

```
$ awk -f vh.awk search=packt virtualhost.conf
```

We can see this more clearly by looking at the command and the output that is produced in the following screenshot:

```
centos6 ~ $ awk -f vh.awk search=packt virtualhost.conf
<VirtualHost *:80>
DocumentRoot /www/packt
ServerName www.packtpub.com
# Other directives here
</VirtualHost>
centos6 ~ $ 
```

XML catalog

We can extend this further into XML files where we may not want to display the complete record, but just certain fields. Consider the following product catalog:

```
<products>
<product>
<name>drill</name>
<price>99</price>
```

```
<stock>5</stock>
</product>

<product>
<name>hammer</name>
<price>10</price>
<stock>50</stock>
</product>

<product>
<name>screwdriver</name>
<price>5</price>
<stock>51</stock>
</product>

<product>
<name>table saw</name>
<price>1099.99</price>
<stock>5</stock>
</product>
</products>
```

Logically, each record is delimited as before with the empty line. Each field though is a little more detailed and we need to use the delimiter as follows: FS="[><]". We define either the opening or closing angle bracket as the field delimiter.

To help analyze this, we can print a single record as follows:

```
<product><name>top</name><price>9</price><stock>5</stock></product>
```

Each angle brace is a field separator, which means that we will have some empty fields. We could rewrite this line as a CSV file:

```
,product,,name,top,/name,,price,9,/price,,stock,5,/stock,,/product,
```

We just replace each angle bracket with a comma; in this way it is more easily read by us. We can see that the content of field 5 is the top value.

Of course, we will not edit the XML file, we will leave it in the XML format. The conversion here is just to highlight how the field separators can be read.

The control file that we use to extract data from the XML file is illustrated in the following code example:

```
BEGIN { FS="[><]"; RS="\n\n" ; OFS=""; }
$0 ~ search { print $4 ": " $5, $8 ": " $9, $12 ": " $13 }
```

Within the `BEGIN` code block, we set the `FS` and `RS` variables as we have discussed. We also set the **Output Field Separator** (`OFS`) or to a space. In this way, when we print the fields we separate the values with a space rather than leaving in the angle brackets. The range makes use of the same match as we used before when looking at the virtual hosts.

If we need to search for the product drill from within the `catalog`, we can use the command in the following example:

```
$ awk -f catalog.awk search=drill catalog.xml
```

The following screenshot shows the output in detail:

```
centos6 ~ $ awk -f catalog.awk search=drill catalog.xml
name: drill price: 99 stock: 5
centos6 ~ $
```

We have now been able to take a rather messy XML file and create readable reports from the catalog. The power of AWK is highlighted again and, for us, the last time within this book. By now, I hope you too can start to make use of this on a regular basis.

Summary

We had three chapters where we used AWK, starting with some basic usage statements in `Chapter 10`, *AWK Fundamentals* where we became comfortable with AWK. In `Chapter 12`, *Summarizing Logs with AWK*, and this chapter, we started building our bespoke applications.

Specifically, in this chapter we saw how we could create reports from the output of standard commands, such as `lastlog`. We saw that we could negate ranges and additionally make use of the `OR` statement. We then built an application that will allow us to query XML data.

For the next two chapters, we will move away from shell scripts and look at scripts using perl and Python so we can compare these scripting languages and make appropriate choices.

Questions

1. How do we get the users who never logged into the system?
2. From the previous question, how do you count the number of users who never logged in?
3. How many lines will be printed from the following command?

Further reading

Please see the following for further reading relating to this chapter:

- https://linux.die.net/man/8/lastlog
- https://en.wikipedia.org/wiki/Lastlog

14
Using Python as a Bash Scripting Alternative

In the previous chapter, we saw a practical example of using AWK and we saw how to process `lastlog` output to produce better reports. In this chapter, we will take a look at another scripting alternative for bash. We will talk about Python. Python is another scripting language and the newest that we have looked at so far. Similar to bash, Python is an interpreted language and makes use of the shebang. Although it does not have a shell interface, we can access a console called REPL where we can type Python code to interact with the system. In this chapter, we will cover the following topics:

- What is Python?
- Saying Hello World the Python way
- Pythonic arguments
- Significant whitespace
- Reading user input
- String manipulation

Technical requirements

The source code for this chapter can be downloaded here:

```
https://github.com/PacktPublishing/Mastering-Linux-Shell-Scripting-Second-
Edition/tree/master/Chapter14
```

What is Python?

Python is an object-oriented interpreted language that is designed to be easy to use and to aid **Rapid Application Development**. This is achieved by the use of simplified semantics in the language.

Python was created at the end of the 1980s, towards the very end of December 1989, by the Dutch developer Guido van Rossum. The majority of the design of the language aims for clarity and simplicity, and one of the main rules of the *Zen of Python* is:

There should be one, and preferable only one, obvious way to do it.

Often systems will have both Python 2 and Python 3 installed; however, all newer distributions are switching to Python 3. We will be working with Python 3.

Since we are using Linux Mint, it comes shipped with Python 3 already.

If you are using another Linux distribution or Python 3 is not found for any reason, you can install it like this:

- On RedHat based distributions:

  ```
  $ sudo yum install python36
  ```

- On Debian based distributions:

  ```
  $ sudo apt-get install python3.6
  ```

Although there is no shell, we can interact with Python using REPL—read, evaluate, print, and loop. We can access this by typing `python3` in the command line or `python36` if you are using CentOS 7. You should see something similar to the following screenshot:

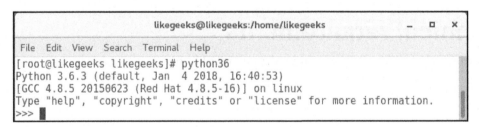

We can see that we are presented with the >>> prompt and this is known as the REPL console. We should emphasize that this is a scripting language and, like bash and Perl, we will normally execute code through the text files that we create. Those text files will normally be expected to have a .py suffix to their name.

While working with REPL, we can print the version independently by importing a module. In Perl, we will use the keyword; in bash we will use the command source; and in Python we use import:

```
>>>import sys
```

With the module loaded, we can now investigate the object-oriented nature of Python by printing the version:

```
>>> sys.version
```

We will navigate to the `sys` object within our namespace and call the version method from that object.

Combining these two commands, we should see the following output:

```
>>> import sys
>>> sys.version
'3.2.3 (default, Mar  1 2013, 11:53:50) \n[GCC 4.6.3]'
>>>
```

To close this section describing Python, we should take a look at the Zen of Python. From REPL, we can type `import this`, as shown in the following screenshot:

```
>>> import this
The Zen of Python, by Tim Peters

Beautiful is better than ugly.
Explicit is better than implicit.
Simple is better than complex.
Complex is better than complicated.
Flat is better than nested.
Sparse is better than dense.
Readability counts.
Special cases aren't special enough to break the rules.
Although practicality beats purity.
Errors should never pass silently.
Unless explicitly silenced.
In the face of ambiguity, refuse the temptation to guess.
There should be one-- and preferably only one --obvious way to do it.
Although that way may not be obvious at first unless you're Dutch.
Now is better than never.
Although never is often better than *right* now.
If the implementation is hard to explain, it's a bad idea.
If the implementation is easy to explain, it may be a good idea.
Namespaces are one honking great idea -- let's do more of those!
>>>
```

This is far more than just the Zen of Python; it's actually a good rule for all programming languages and a guide for developers.

Finally, to close the REPL, we will use *Ctrl + D* in Linux or *Ctrl + Z* in Windows.

Saying Hello World the Python way

The code we write in Python should be clear and uncluttered: sparse is better than dense. We will need the shebang on the first line and then the `print` statement. The `print` function includes the newline and we do not need semicolons at the end of the line. We can see the edited version of `$HOME/bin/hello.py` in the following example:

```
#!/usr/bin/python3
print("Hello World")
```

We will still need to add the execute permission, but we can run the code as earlier using `chmod`. This is shown in the following command but we should be a little used to this now:

```
$ chmod u+x $HOME/bin/hello.py
```

Finally, we can now execute the code to see our greeting.

Similarly, you can run the file using the Python interpreter from the command line like this:

```
$ python3 $HOME/bin/hello.py
```

Or in some Linux distributions, you can run it like this:

```
$ python36 $HOME/bin/hello.py
```

Again, knowing at least one language makes it easier to adapt to others and there aren't many new features in this.

Pythonic arguments

We should know by now that we will want to pass command-line arguments to Python and we can do this using the `argv` array. However, we are more like bash; with Python we combine the program name into the array with the other arguments.

Python also uses lowercase instead of uppercase in the object name:

- The `argv` array is a part of the `sys` object
- `sys.argv[0]` is the script name
- `sys.argv[1]` is the first argument supplied to the script
- `sys.argv[2]` is the second supplied argument and so on
- The argument count will always be at least 1, so, keep this in mind when checking for supplied arguments

Supplying arguments

If we create the `$HOME/bin/args.py` file we can see this in action. The file should be created as follows and made executable:

```
#!/usr/bin/python3
import sys
print("Hello " + sys.argv[1])
```

If we run the script with a supplied argument, we should see something similar to the following screenshot:

```
pi@pilabs ~/bin $ ./args.py fred
Hello fred
pi@pilabs ~/bin $ _
```

Our code is still quite clean and simple; however, you may have noticed that we cannot combine the quoted text in the `print` statement with the argument. We use the + symbol to join or concatenate the two strings together. As there is no specific symbol to denote a variable or any other type of object, they cannot appear as static text within quotes.

Counting arguments

As previously mentioned, the script name is the first argument at index 0 of the array. So, if we try to count the arguments, then the count should always be at the very least 1. In other words, if we have not supplied arguments, the argument count will be 1. To count the items in an array, we can use the `len()` function.

If we edit the script to include a new line we will see this work, as follows:

```
#!/usr/bin/python3
import sys
print("Hello " + sys.argv[1])
print( "length is: " + str(len(sys.argv)) )
```

Executing the code as we have earlier, we can see that we have supplied two arguments—the script name and then the string Mokhtar:

If we try and have a single print statement to print the output and the number of arguments, then it will produce an error because we can't concatenate integers with strings. The length value is an integer and this cannot be mixed with strings without conversion. That's why we used the str function to convert the integer to a string. The following code will fail:

```
#!/usr/bin/python3
import sys
print("Hello " + sys.argv[1] + " " + len(sys.argv))
```

If we try to run the script and omit to supply an argument, then there will be a null value in the array when we reference index 1. This will give an error, as shown in the following screenshot:

```
pi@pilabs ~/bin $ ./args.py
Traceback (most recent call last):
  File "./args.py", line 3, in <module>
    print("Hello " + sys.argv[1] + " " + str(len(sys.argv)))
IndexError: list index out of range
pi@pilabs ~/bin $ _
```

We of course need to handle this to prevent the error; enter the concept of significant whitespace.

Significant whitespace

A major difference between Python and most other languages is that additional whitespace can mean something. The indent level of your code defines the block of code to which it belongs. So far, we have not indented the code we have created past the start of the line. This means that all of the code is at the same indent level and belongs to the same code block. Rather than using brace brackets or the do and done keywords to define the code block, we use indents. If we indent with two or four spaces or even tabs, then we must stick to those spaces or tabs. When we return to the previous indent level, we return to the previous code block.

This seems complex but it is really quite simple and keeps your code clean and uncluttered. If we edit the `arg.py` file to prevent unwelcomed errors, if an argument is not supplied, we can see this in action:

```
#!/usr/bin/python3
import sys
count = len(sys.argv)
if ( count > 1 ):
    print("Arguments supplied: " + str(count))
    print("Hello " + sys.argv[1])
print("Exiting " + sys.argv[0])
```

The `if` statement checks if the argument count is greater than 1 or not. We now store for ease, the argument count has its own variable, which we call `count`. The code block starts with the colon and then all of the following code that is indented with four spaces is part of the code that will execute when the condition returns to true.

When we return to the previous indent level, we return to the main code block and we execute the code regardless of the status of the condition.

We can see this illustrated in the following screenshot, where we can execute the script with and without the argument:

```
pi@pilabs ~/bin $ ./args.py
Exiting ./args.py
pi@pilabs ~/bin $ ./args.py fred
Arguments supplied: 2
Hello fred
Exiting ./args.py
```

Reading user input

If we want the welcome message to greet us by name, no matter whether we supply the argument to the script or not, we can add in a prompt to capture the data while the script is running. Python makes this simple and easy to implement. We can see, from the edited file shown in the screenshot that follows, how this is achieved:

```
#!/usr/bin/python3
import sys
count = len(sys.argv)
name = ''

if ( count == 1 ):
    name = input("Enter a name: ")
else:
    name = sys.argv[1]

print("Hello " + name)
print("Exiting " + sys.argv[0])
```

We make use of a new variable in the script that we set in the main block, initially, to be an empty string. We set it here to make the variable available to the complete script and all code blocks:

```
likegeeks@likegeeks-VirtualBox ~/Desktop                    — + ✕
File  Edit  View  Search  Terminal  Help
likegeeks@likegeeks-VirtualBox ~/Desktop $ ./args.py Mokhtar
Hello Mokhtar
Exiting ./args.py
likegeeks@likegeeks-VirtualBox ~/Desktop $ ./args.py
Enter a name: Mokhtar
Hello Mokhtar
Exiting ./args.py
likegeeks@likegeeks-VirtualBox ~/Desktop $
```

The `input` function in Python 3 (or `raw_input` in Python 2) can be used to get user input. We store that input in the `name` variable. If we have supplied an argument we pick it up on the code in the `else` block and set the `name` variable to the first supplied argument. It is this that is used in the `print` statement back in the main block.

Using Python to write to files

To add some variety to this chapter, we will now look at printing this data to a file. Again using Python, this is quite a simple and easy way to pick up. We will start by making a copy of our existing `args.py`. We will copy this to `$HOME/bin/file.py`. The new `file.py` should read similar to the following screenshot and have the execute permission set:

```python
#!/usr/bin/python3
import sys
count = len(sys.argv)
name = ''

if ( count == 1 ):
    name = input("Enter a name: ")
else:
    name = sys.argv[1]

log = open("/tmp/script.log","a")
log.write("Hello " + name + "\n")
log.close()
```

You will notice that we have just altered the final lines and instead of print we now open a file. We also see more of the object-orientated nature of Python, whereby it dynamically assigns the `write()` and `close()` methods to the object log, as it is seen as an instance of a file. When we open the file, we open it up for the purpose of appending, meaning that we do not overwrite the existing content if it is already there. If the file is not there, we will create a new file. If we use `w`, we will open the file for writing, which might translate to overwriting, so take care.

You can see that this is an easy task; this is why Python is used in many applications and is taught widely in schools.

String manipulation

Dealing with strings in Python is very simple: you can search, replace, change character case, and perform other manipulations with ease:

To search for a string, you can use the find method like this:

```
#!/usr/bin/python3
str = "Welcome to Python scripting world"
print(str.find("scripting"))
```

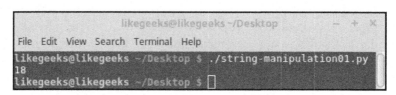

The string count in Python starts from zero too, so the position of the word scripting is at 18.

You can get a specific substring using square brackets like this:

```
#!/usr/bin/python3
str = "Welcome to Python scripting world"
print(str[:2]) # Get the first 2 letters (zero based)
print(str[2:]) # Start from the second letter
print(str[3:5]) # from the third to fifth letter
print(str[-1]) # -1 means the last letter if you don't know the length
```

To replace a string, you can use the replace method like this:

```
#!/usr/bin/python3
str = "Welcome to Python scripting world"
str2 = str.replace("Python", "Shell")
print(str2)
```

To change the character case, you can use `upper()` and `lower()` functions:

As you can see, working with strings in Python is very simple. Python as an alternative scripting language is an awesome choice.

The power of Python lies in the libraries available out there. Literally, there are thousands of libraries for everything you can imagine.

Summary

This now finishes our look at Python and it certainly has been a brief tour. We can again emphasize the similarities that you will see in many languages and the importance of learning any coding language. What you learn in one language will help in most other languages that you come across.

What we learn from the Zen of Python will help us design and develop great code. We can print the Zen of Python using the following Python code:

```
>>>import this
```

We can type the code on the REPL prompt. Keeping your code clean and well spaced-out will aid readability and ultimately this will help with code maintenance.

We have also seen that Python likes you to be explicit in your code and will not implicitly convert data types.

Finally, we saw how to manipulate strings using Python.

We are also at the end of the book but hopefully, the start of your scripting career. Good luck and thank you for reading.

Questions

1. How many characters will be printed from the following code?

   ```
   #!/usr/bin/python3
   str = "Testing Python.."
   print(str[8:])
   ```

2. How many words will be printed from the following code?

   ```
   #!/usr/bin/python3
   print( len(sys.argv) )
   Solution: Nothing
   ```

3. How many words will be printed from the following code?

   ```
   #!/usr/bin/python3
   import sys
   print("Hello " + sys.argv[-1])
   ```

Further reading

Please see the following for further reading relating to this chapter:

- https://www.python.org/about/gettingstarted/
- https://docs.python.org/3/

Assessments

Chapter 1

1. The error is in the second line: There should be no spaces in the variable declaration.

   ```
   #!/bin/bash
   var1="Welcome to bash scripting ..."
   echo $var1
   ```

2. The result will be `Tuesday` because the array is zero based.
3. There are two errors here: the first error is the space in the variable declaration and the second error is the usage of single quotes where we should use backticks instead.

   Solution:

   ```
   #!/bin/bash files='ls -la' echo $files
   ```

4. The value of `b` variable will be `c` and the value of `c` will be `a`.

   Since we didn't use dollar signs in the assignment lines, the variable will take the character value instead of the integer value.

Chapter 2

1. Three

   This is because the whole bash shebang is primarily a comment, so there are three lines of comment.

2. There is no space between the option `-b` and its value, so it will be treated as an option.

   ```
   -a
   -b50
   -c
   ```

3. 1

   Four

   This is because we have five passed parameters and we use the shift to drop a parameter.

4. 2

   `-n`

   This is because it's on the left and the `shift` command drops parameters from the left.

Chapter 3

1. `False`

   Since lower-case characters have a higher ASCII order, the statement will return `False`.

2. Both are correct and will return the same result, which is `Strings` are not identical.

3. `Three`

   We can use the following:

   - `-ge`: Greater than or equal to
   - `-gt`: Greater than
   - `-ne`: Not equal to

4. True

   Since one test is enough to return true, so we can be sure that the second test will return true.

Chapter 4

1. We can make the following changes :

```
"Hello message": {
    "prefix": "hello",
    "body": [
      "echo 'Hello ${1|first,second,third|}' "
    ],
    "description": "Hello message"
  }
```

2. The `source` command.

Chapter 5

1. By using `((`:

```
#!/bin/bash
num=$(( 25 - 8 ))
echo $num
```

2. The problem is with the space in the filename. To fix it, put the filename between quotes:

```
$ rm "my file"
```

3. There is no dollar sign before the parentheses:

```
#!/bin/bash
a=$(( 8 + 4 ))
echo $a
```

Chapter 6

1. No lines. Since the loop output is redirected to a file, nothing will appear on the screen.
2. Four. The loop will start at 8 and continue until it reaches 12, it will match the condition which is greater than or equal, and it will break the loop.

3. The problem is with the comma in the `for` loop definition. It should be semicolon instead. So the correct script should be as follows:

```
#!/bin/bash
for (( v=1; v <= 10; v++ ))
do
echo "value is $v"
done
```

4. Since the decrement statement is outside the loop, the count variable will be the same value, which is 10. It's an endless loop, it will print 10 forever, and to stop it, you need to press *Ctrl + C*.

Chapter 7

1. Since we used the $1 variable not $@, the function will return the first element only.
2. 50. Yes, it's a global variable, but because we printed the value before the function call, the variable isn't affected.
3. Missing brackets () or adding the keyword function before the function name. It should be written like this:

```
clean_file() {
    is_file "$1"
    BEFORE=$(wc -l "$1")
    echo "The file $1 starts with $BEFORE"
    sed -i.bak '/^\s*#/d;/^$/d' "$1"
    AFTER=$(wc -l "$1")
    echo "The file $1 is now $AFTER"
}
```

4. The problem is in the function call. We shouldn't use brackets () during a function call. Brackets should only be used in function definitions. The correct code will be like this:

```
#!/bin/bash
myfunc() {
arr=$@
echo "The array from inside the function: ${arr[*]}"
}
```

```
test_arr=(1 2 3)
echo "The origianl array is: ${test_arr[*]}"
myfunc ${test_arr[*]}
```

Chapter 8

1. None. Because you are searching for Sed with a capital letter which does not exist
2. None. The delete command d only deletes lines from the stream, not the file. To delete from the file, you can use the -i option.
3. Fourth line. Because we used append command **a**, it will be inserted after the specified position.
4. None, because the w flag is only used with the substitute command s.

Chapter 9

1. You can use the following command to print line number 50:

   ```
   $ sed -n '50 p ' /etc/httpd/conf/httpd.conf
   ```

2. You can use following command to change Apache default port 80 to 8080:

   ```
   $ sed -i '0,/Listen [0-9]*/s//Listen 8080/'
   /etc/httpd/conf/httpd.conf
   ```

   We search for Listen, where it defines the Apache default port, search for the number beside it, and change it to Listen 8080.

Chapter 10

1. Nothing

   You should use the variable name without the dollar sign to print it.

2. Solution: zero

   Because you should print $1 instead of $2 where $1 is the first field.

3. The `while` loop should iterate with `i` value less than 4 not 3.

4. 1

Because the only user that has UID less than 1 is root (`UID=0`), so one line will be printed.

Chapter 11

1. 0 lines

Because there is a period after the word `awesome`, if you want to print that line, you can use the following command:

```
$ awk '/awesome\.$/{print $0}' myfile
```

2. 2 lines

Since we search for the line that contains the word `scripting`. With a period after it followed by any text, this pattern only exists in two lines because the third line doesn't contain a period after the word.

3. 3 lines

As we used the question mark that means the character class is not a must for the pattern to match.

4. Nothing

As we used the pipe symbol, which is an ERE character, and as we used sed, we must use the `-r` option for sed to turn the extended engine on.

Chapter 12

1. Field 1
2. You can use `print NR` or alternatively pipe the output to `wc -l`

   We must use `-l` otherwise, it will count words instead.

   ```
   $ awk '{print $1}' access.log | sort | uniq -c
   ```

   ```
   $ awk '{print $7}' access.log | grep 'php' | sort | uniq -c | sort
   -nr | head -n 1
   ```

   You should use head `-n 1` to get the one page only.

Chapter 13

1. Use the `lastlog` command

   ```
   $ lastlog | awk ' /Never logged/ { print $1}'
   ```

2. Use the `wc` command

   ```
   $ lastlog | awk ' /Never logged/ { print $1}' | wc -l
   ```

3. Zero. Because the line ends with two asterisks.

Chapter 14

1. 8
2. Since we are using the `sys` module, we should import it first.

   So the correct code should look like this:

   ```
   #!/usr/bin/python3
   import sys
   print( len(sys.argv))
   ```

3. 2

Other Books You May Enjoy

If you enjoyed this book, you may be interested in these other books by Packt:

Mastering Linux Security and Hardening
Donald A. Tevault

ISBN: 978-1-78862-030-7

- Use various techniques to prevent intruders from accessing sensitive data
- Prevent intruders from planting malware, and detect whether malware has been planted
- Prevent insiders from accessing data that they aren't authorized to access
- Do quick checks to see whether a computer is running network services that it doesn't need to run
- Learn security techniques that are common to all Linux distros, and some that are distro-specific

Linux Shell Scripting Cookbook
Clif Flynt, Sarath Lakshman, Shantanu Tushar

ISBN: 978-1-78588-198-5

- Interact with websites via scripts
- Write shell scripts to mine and process data from the Web
- Automate system backups and other repetitive tasks with crontab
- Create, compress, and encrypt archives of your critical data.
- Configure and monitor Ethernet and wireless networks
- Monitor and log network and system activity
- Tune your system for optimal performance
- Improve your system's security
- Identify resource hogs and network bottlenecks
- Extract audio from video files
- Create web photo albums
- Use git or fossil to manage revision control and interact with FOSS projects
- Create and maintain Linux containers and Virtual Machines
- Run a private Cloud server

Leave a review - let other readers know what you think

Please share your thoughts on this book with others by leaving a review on the site that you bought it from. If you purchased the book from Amazon, please leave us an honest review on this book's Amazon page. This is vital so that other potential readers can see and use your unbiased opinion to make purchasing decisions, we can understand what our customers think about our products, and our authors can see your feedback on the title that they have worked with Packt to create. It will only take a few minutes of your time, but is valuable to other potential customers, our authors, and Packt. Thank you!

Index

L

M

N

O

P

Made in the USA
Coppell, TX
29 December 2022

10005160R00157